The Sound
of
Reformation

Garris Elkins

The Sound of Reformation
© 2017 Garris Elkins

Prophetic Horizons
PO Box 509, Jacksonville, OR, 97530 USA
info@prophetichorizons.com | www.GarrisElkins.com

ISBN-13: 978-0692884423
ISBN-10: 0692884424

A WELL-DESERVED THANKS

When I wrote the rough draft of *The Sound of Reformation*, I basically assembled my notes and research and asked my wife, Jan, to help me sort them all out. For every hour I spent writing this book, Jan spent at least two reorganizing my thinking to give the book a sense of flow. I am truly grateful for her act of love.

And to Anna, my favorite editor—thank you. You walked me through the creation of all my books. You have provided wise counsel and great encouragement. I so agree with a recent assessment of your editing skills from one of your other authors, "The editing is strong with this one."

CONTENTS

DEDICATION

This book is dedicated to everyone who is uncomfortable settling in to what has been and what is at the expense of what can be. If you are willing to walk with humility and ask for wisdom, you will see the great things God has planned for His Church and for each culture on the face of the Earth.

Thanks for taking this journey with me. It is an honor to walk with you in this time of reformation, discovering aspects of God our generation desperately needs to see and experience. These changes might seem new or radical to us, but reformation by definition re-forms the status quo. How these changes are expressed will be a conduit for the greater glory of God. To make Him famous is part of our destiny.

You have been prepared for such a time as this. You have matured in your love, and now love compels you to make a sound—to speak the truth in love.

Suddenly, there was a sound from heaven...
—Acts 2:2

A FIRST WORD

The Sound of Reformation began to take shape as a book while I prepared to teach on reformation at a regional conference. My ideas about reformation have been influenced by our collective Church history, especially the Protestant Reformation that took place 500 years ago in Europe. (In fact, as I write this, it is the year of the 500th anniversary of that Reformation.)

When Jan and I lived in Berlin, Germany, we took several day trips to Wittenberg and stood before the door upon which Martin Luther nailed his 95 theses. I always appreciated Luther's boldness in proclaiming what he discovered in Scripture: forgotten truths lost to the Church. Luther had to nail his thoughts to the outside of the church door because those on the inside were not yet ready to welcome the Reformation.

Luther could not know the long-range outcome of his actions. From where he stood in history, he would experience a great deal of upheaval and backlash. And he didn't get everything right; he only had snapshots of a much larger picture. But with the revelation Luther possessed, he was able to set in motion the historic Reformation that would change how we see the Church.

Reformers are currently nailing the demands for transformation to the door of our current expression of the Church. These reformers are not the enemy. They are prophets announcing the way forward. Leave the sanctuary of the status quo and bravely go to the front door of your spiritual experience. Read what the reformers have posted. What they are asking us to consider will reveal our future and eventually, it will become the record of our history.

Major reformation in the Church must take place from time to time in order to restore original truth and to help keep us in pace with the expanding revelation of God. Reformation is never a one-time event. A living faith must reform if it is to grow and have a continual Kingdom impact in every sphere of culture.

It is becoming clear to me the next reformation of the Church will not take place inside the church structure or institution, though we will use the five-fold gifts that have been nurtured in the Church. The reformation will take place across all the mountains of cultural influence—between people in moments of human interaction in the marketplace, in homes, in city council chambers, in corporate board rooms, in big-box store break rooms, and everyplace where a follower of Jesus walks. The hallmark of the coming reformation will be simplicity. God is about to downsize the Church to remove the accumulated clutter around our faith in preparation for a return to the supernatural simplicity of our mission.

ONE

The Flight of Faith

Flying taught me a lot about life. As a young pastor, I also worked as a flight instructor. I taught new pilots and worked as an instrument instructor, teaching advanced students how to fly through inclement weather using only their instruments for navigation.

On one such instructional flight, I had my student depart the Newport, Oregon airport for a night flight to Portland. We had to navigate through a layer of clouds on departure, and the same condition was waiting for us at our destination.

As soon as we took off, we were immediately in the clouds. The city lights of Newport quickly dissolved beneath us, and we entered complete darkness, fully enveloped in clouds. The glow of our instrument panel was the only visible light. I instructed my student to make sure he transitioned to his instruments as soon as he got airborne so he would be flying by them when we entered the clouds. A few minutes later, we were greeted by a full moon and clear skies when we broke through the top of the cloud layer.

The moon illuminated the clouds that were now below us, and the light reflecting off of them was almost as bright as day. It was beautifully surreal. We droned along with the huge moon overhead and a bright pillow of moonlit clouds below. It was a magical flight to Portland. As we approached the airport, my student used the same instruments that got us on top of the clouds to begin our descent through the clouds to land safely in Portland. For the entire flight, my student followed a flight path using only his instruments to navigate.

Flying by instruments can trigger a variety of emotions and reactions in a student. These must be overcome to maintain safe and steady flight. In instrument conditions, pilots can experience something called vertigo. Vertigo happens when a pilot no longer has a horizon line to focus on. It is a very strange sensation. You can actually feel like you are flying upside down when you are right-side up. You must trust your instruments, not your feelings.

I prefer to fly in clear air. I love to look out over great distances to see the beauty of an expansive landscape. I also feel more secure being able to see the Earth below and any available airstrips, roads, or even an open field should I need to make an emergency landing.

We all want to see the way made clear before we step into the newness of God's leadings. Following the nudges of the Spirit doesn't always feel logical. Flying without our normal points of reference stirs up all kinds of nervous and resistant reactions, and so will a life of faith. There is always uncertainty at life junctures when faith calls us to fly into the unknown.

This is the essence of reformation; our instruments of faith tell us to hold a particular heading that will deliver us into a future we do not yet see. Reformation is waiting ahead of us through the clouds and darkness of our current understanding of the Church and its role in culture.

We have entered the clouds of transition. Instrument pilots experience a transition when they move their point of reference from the visible horizon line outside the aircraft to the instruments inside the cockpit. Just as I told my student right before he entered the clouds for that night flight, we need to transition to the instruments of faith before we enter the clouds of reformation. If we are not flying by faith before we enter the clouds, the disapproval and doubt that will surely surround us will overcome our ability to navigate safely because we will have become disoriented.

Get on your instruments of faith now and keep flying. God will show you vistas of spiritual beauty that are invisible until you rise above your current line of sight and see what God has planned for the future of the Church.

Repositioned for Joy

We all want a simple faith that works in real life. This is the kind of faith that inspired the twelve disciples to walk right by the religious establishment of their day, not wanting any part of the complicated and life-draining expression of religion offered by the scribes, Sadducees, and Pharisees.

The disciples wanted to walk with Jesus because He was real and life giving. He pierced their spirits with His love. He demonstrated the Kingdom of God with His power. He was comfortable to be around. These followers of Jesus would have been uncomfortable if Jesus asked them to wear the complicated garments of religion—garments that would never fit, no matter how many alterations. The real Jesus always fits.

I have ridden a bicycle all my life. Many times I will get on my bike to clear my head and simply unwind. It is my mobile refuge.

When I got close to sixty years of age, I needed to make a change. I still wanted to ride, but not on the type of bikes I had ridden for years. Those bikes are the diamond-frame ones most of us are used to seeing. The diamond shape is formed by the frame tubing that links the handlebars, seat, and pedal mechanism.

My diamond-frame bike began to be increasingly uncomfortable. I tried padded handlebars and padded gloves, but my wrists still hurt. I tried expensive leather seats anatomically designed to relieve pressure points, but my rear-end still got sore. After an hour on a diamond-frame bike my neck would begin to ache. I was about to give up riding when I discovered another kind of bike. It is called a recumbent bicycle.

A recumbent gives the rider an entirely new posture and riding experience. You are still riding a bike, but the unique design relieves all the normal pressure points and pain and gives you back the joy of riding.

On a recumbent it looks like you are reclining in a lounge chair peddling with your feet out in front of you. At first, I thought these bikes were a quirky fad until I took one for a test ride. I was hooked. I began to scour online ads for a used recumbent. One day, there it was: my recumbent. I contacted the seller and made the purchase.

As soon as I got my new bike home, I took off for a ride along the country roads and through the farmland surrounding the small town where I live. It felt like I had died and gone to bike heaven. I was no longer riding bent over the handlebars; instead, I was reclining, so my neck no longer hurt.

This new posture affected something else: my line of vision. I could actually see my surroundings from my laid-back posture. I wasn't always looking down at the moving pavement or straining to look up. The sore wrists were gone because I was no longer continually putting pressure on them. My backside was singing the hallelujah chorus because the wide, nylon-webbed seat spread out my point of contact with the bike. No more pain!

It you were to walk into our garage, you would see my old diamond frame bike hanging on the garage wall gathering dust. It has been hanging there for the last several years since the recumbent arrived. A year ago, I took it out for ride just to see if I noticed a difference. After a few miles, I was dying. My sore wrists came back to say hello, along with their traveling companions—a sore neck and an aching rear-end.

I cut the ride short and returned home to hang the diamond frame bike back on the garage wall where it has remained ever since.

Reformation will give us an opportunity to make an exchange: we exchange what no longer works and actually causes a lot of pain and trouble for something new and refreshing—something we actually want to ride. When I first thought of making the change from a diamond-frame bike to a recumbent, I was a bit concerned. Would I like it? Would it be a waste of money? Once I rode the recumbent, all those concerns melted away.

After that exchange, I was still biking, but in a different way. Sometimes, to keep moving forward, we will need to change the way we ride so that we can endure the long haul of life.

The discovery of a new perspective can bring joy. You can leave behind a way of life that produces a painful misrepresentation of God and His Kingdom. In doing so, you will become a rolling advertisement of something wonderful. The expression of joy on your face will become an invitation for other people to dismount from religious vehicles of pain to experience the new and good thing God is doing. The exchange is ours to make.

Creating Order with Sound

Any creative moment in human history can trace its origin back to the sounds of Creation when God breathed into a formless, dark, and empty place. He spoke, and the Earth was transformed into a habitation suitable for human life.

God created human life forms in the image of Himself, the Creator. He gave us a will: the ability to make choices. Giving us a will was an act of true love, devoid of control and manipulation. The risk of a free will is that love can be received or refused. When our ancestors chose death over life, death entered all of creation. Down through the ages, the sons and daughters of God have used their free will to create both life and death.

Humanity, described as the masterpiece of God, was restored to God's original plan through Jesus Christ, the Second Adam. Rule and authority was also restored and destiny was reinstated. Through His death and resurrection, Jesus made a way for us to be born as new creations.

After the resurrection of Jesus, the disciples were meeting behind locked doors because they were afraid of the Jewish leaders. Jesus suddenly appeared and stood before them:

> *"Peace be with you"' he said. As he spoke, he showed them the wounds in his hands and his side. They were filled with joy when they saw the Lord! Again he said, "Peace be with you. As the Father has sent me, so I am sending you." Then he breathed on them and said, "Receive the Holy Spirit. If you forgive anyone's sins, they are*

forgiven. If you do not forgive them, they are not forgiven" (John 20: 19b-23).

A new creation took place for the second time in human history. What failed with Adam was restored in Jesus. When Jesus breathed into His disciples, the Spirit took up permanent residence in human beings for the first time in human history. They would become what Paul later described as new creations: "anyone who belongs to Christ has become a new person. The old is gone; a new life has begun" (II Corinthians 5:17).

At Creation the breath of God reformed the formless mass of elements and turned them into planet Earth. That same breath of God formed Adam and every living organism and life-system.

Throughout all of history and in this moment of time, it is the sound created by the breath of God that releases new life. All creation and every reformation began with the sound of God's breath—His word spoken into dark and void places, creating new life and new direction.

The Sound of Reformation

These new, Spirit-indwelled disciples came to the Day of Pentecost in obedience to the marching orders Jesus had given them. On that day, a new sound was released: "Suddenly, there was a sound from heaven..." (Acts 2:2).

The word translated as sound here is *ēchos:* it means sound or noise (and is also the root of the English word "echo"). The same word was used in Luke 4 to describe the sound of a testimony created by the ministry of Jesus when a demon possessed man was set free. It was also used in Hebrews 12 to describe the sound of a ram's horn trumpeting the Israelites to attention to hear the word of the Lord.

That root word *ēchos* also forms the verb, *ēchéō,* which means *to sound* or *roar* and is found in I Corinthians 13:1 where Paul is defining love to the Corinthians: "If I could speak all the languages of earth and of angels, but didn't love others, I would only be a noisy gong or a clanging cymbal."

The Church has been called to make the sound of love that will echo through each sphere of cultural influence. The rest of Acts 2:2 reveals more of that sound: "Suddenly, there was a sound from heaven like the roaring of a mighty windstorm."

It was not a windstorm. It was *like* a windstorm. Those present described it as an otherworldly event. It was similar to John on the Isle of Patmos trying to use first-century language to describe futuristic events. At some point, words will fail to describe the new thing God is doing. Even in our day, what is coming will be described *like* something familiar to us, but it will actually be beyond our ability to describe.

The wind of Pentecost created a noise so loud, it got the attention of an entire city. Acts 2:6 tell us, "When they heard the loud noise, everyone came running...." This is the value of unusual phenomena; it gets the attention of culture. If you want a suddenly of God without phenomena, you may keep yourself from receiving your promise. You might actually distance yourself from the very thing God wants you to receive.

On the Day of Pentecost, those who were uncomfortable with the unusual events ridiculed them. The critics of Pentecost said, "They're just drunk, that's all!" If we choose to not experience God beyond our familiar and restricted understanding of Him, we limit ourselves with the equivalent of "that's all!" Disbelief parks us at the border of our dismissive reasoning and leaves us unchanged—even while change is taking place all around us. God never promised that reformation would be comfortable or familiar or fully definable.

The Message of Reformation

I have come to believe the hinge point for understanding the events on the Day of Pentecost is found in Acts 2:11: "And we all hear these people speaking in our own languages about the wonderful things God has done!" This was the testimony of those who heard a noise that sounded like *the roaring of a mighty windstorm*. The city came running to that sound and heard the message of God's goodness carried on the wind of the Spirit.

Understanding the content of the message of Pentecost is critical if we are going to know what it means to speak the truth in love to the people who live in our world. I believe the message of Pentecost announced the wonderful things God has done. The content of those words would sound a lot like Isaiah 61:1-3:

> *The Spirit of the Sovereign Lord is upon me,*
> *for the Lord has anointed me*
> *to bring good news to the poor.*
> *He has sent me to comfort the brokenhearted*
> *and to proclaim that captives will be released*
> *and prisoners will be freed.*
>
> *He has sent me to tell those who mourn*
> *that the time of the Lord's favor has come.*
> *And with it, the day of God's anger against their enemies.*
>
> *To all who mourn in Israel:*
> *he will give a crown of beauty for ashes,*
> *a joyous blessing instead of mourning,*

festive praise instead of despair....

The sound of the Spirit ushered in the Good News for the whole world. It was so simple that many of the religious leaders of the day missed the announcement. The Day of Pentecost trumpeted the sound of a reformation that would be heard repeatedly in each chapter of our history as God brings us back to His original intent.

The sound of reformation will draw people in our communities who will marvel at what they hear. It will be a sound made in a familiar language so that they will be able to hear about the wonderful things God has done.

What if it is just that simple? Reformation begins with a sound and a message people can easily understand. God has not made this difficult. *We* have made it difficult, and that is what God plans to reform with a fresh outpouring of His love.

A New Vocabulary for a New Season

Love translated the events that took place on the Day of Pentecost. When God anointed Peter to preach that day, Peter spoke in his own language while empowered by the Spirit. The Holy Spirit interpreted his message to the many nationalities and languages represented in the crowd. Each person was able to hear, in their own language, the wonderful and loving things God had done.

The winds of reformation are blowing once again and will continue to blow long enough to bring about the change God desires. A fully developed reformation will eventually deliver a symphonic sound, heard in every sphere of culture.

That sound will result in expressions of amazing love, where hopelessness and despair have made the loudest noise. The breath of the Spirit will blow away religious obstacles that deafen ears to the message of truth spoken in love. That truth is what we are being equipped to deliver.

Ask God to help you hear the new sounds of His Spirit. He will fill you with wonder and amazement. He will give you an interpretation—delivering to you a miracle of understanding the times in which we live. "Anyone with ears to hear should listen and understand!" (Matthew 11:15).

Bunkers of Fear or Bridges of Hope

I have visited many nations. In the 1990's, I traveled to several Eastern European countries that had only recently emerged from communist rule, including Albania. Today, Albania is reinventing itself through trade, diplomacy, and exposure to the outside world, but it was a closed country for many years.

Under communist rule, Albania was led by Enver Hoxha. Hoxha was a very repressive and paranoid leader who governed one of the most depressed and poverty-stricken nations in Europe. Hoxha used fear to control his people. He tried to convince them they had it so good under his leadership that the outside world was ready to invade Albania at any moment and take away their meager portion.

As a result of that delusion, a campaign was begun to construct defensive concrete bunkers throughout the nation to repel the imaginary horde of invaders. Thousands of these military bunkers were strategically positioned to point outward toward the borders of the nation in preparation for an imminent invasion. In 1983 there were 173,371 of these bunkers in a nation with a landmass approximately the size of New Hampshire. To this day, they are still scattered throughout the landscape of Albania.

When I recall the image of the bunkers I saw in Albania twenty years ago, I am reminded of segments of the Western Church today. There is a great deal of suspicion. Bunkers of distrust and the fear of heresy have been erected to protect our particular version of spiritual reality. The hard walls of these fortified bunkers face outward toward any opposing points of view that would challenge the status quo. They guard against any imagined invasion of new thinking. These bunkers are constructed with the bricks and mortar of well-crafted words empowered by human logic that seek to control much of what we are allowed to believe.

God builds bridges, not bunkers. When fear is allowed to run rampant, we see imaginary enemies everywhere trying to cross our borders and pollute our sense of theological purity. In our nervous faith, we fire warning shots at every moving shadow or unfamiliar sound. Like the abandoned concrete bunkers I saw each time I visited Albania, there will come a day when the remains of our fear will be widely apparent to those who study our history.

A better way of living was offered to the Albanians, and their nation began a process of national reformation. Those who loved Albania helped the nation build a bridge to other cultures and nations. This building began when people made the choice to abandon a siege mentality for free enterprise and free-thinking. The bunkers in Albania now house goats and chickens and provide a place for tourists to take selfies. The structures of fear are decaying reminders of a failed way of life.

The creation of bridges is the first step in reforming a society, but to build a bridge, you need a real and tangible destination on the other side. Some of our bridges have been built to non-existent locations. They were constructed with our opinions and our narrow interpretations of reality. They did not represent the depths of God's heart. These bridges connect to dead-end roads leading nowhere.

Only truth spoken in love can build bridges connecting people to the heart of God. Fear does not have the building materials or plans available for that kind of construction project.

Dead Ends

While on a recent trip, I left my hotel room early one morning to take a walk before I drove on to my next destination. I walked up a residential street and passed a strange little side street with a "Dead End" sign at the edge of the pavement. The street was only about 10 feet long and ended at a cliff. The sign looked like a joke some construction worker had erected, but it was real. I stopped and stood there in amusement, and then the Lord began to speak to me.

I was looking at a plan gone awry. Some builder or city official had announced a development that would never happen. This advertised event had become nothing more than a short, side-street diversion leading to a cliff. It was a waste of time and energy. It was a constant drive-by reminder of what would never happen.

As reformation unfolds, don't be side-tracked by signs of the failed projects of the past. God is not in the business of announcing something and then leading you to a dead-end street sign in some cosmic joke. Whole segments of the Church have parked at these dead-end signs and tried to build their life work without the hope of something new.

Learn from your past, but never allow it to define your future. If you have been diverted down a dead-end street, get back on the main road of faith and keep moving. Dead-end journeys are not part of your assignment or your calling.

David said to God, "You will show me the way of life..." (Psalm 16:11). That promise was sourced in the faithfulness of God to always make His way known to us. That promise is yours to believe.

Revealing the Unknown God

When I began preparing for the conference that would spark the genesis of this book, the Lord took me to Acts 17 where I reread Paul's interaction with the Athenians. Paul stood before the Council of Athens and addressed them with an interesting comment:

> *"Men of Athens, I notice that you are very religious in every way, for as I was walking along I saw your many shrines. And one of your altars had this inscription on it: 'To an Unknown God.' This God, whom you worship without knowing, is the one I'm telling you about" (Acts 17:22b-23).*

Athens was known as the city of 10,000 gods. Just to be safe, the city officials had also erected a statue to an Unknown God to cover all their bases. Paul's ministry in Athens reminds me of what God wants to do through a new wave of reformers.

The Church needs to be introduced to unknown aspects of God's nature. We desperately need greater depth as well as fresh insights. We know God from the aspect of our salvation, but we have so much more of His nature to discover. Religious lies and misunderstandings have often hidden the fullness of God.

The task of a reformer is to remove the barriers that stand in the way of people experiencing the beauty and majesty of God in new and fresh ways. This is a risky experience because what we were relying on for security will be challenged in the process.

Reformation introduces us to the lost parts of our faith originally delivered to the Church, and it introduces us to the God who made that delivery in the person of Jesus Christ. Without a shift in our thinking, we will continue to believe the narrow slice of a previous understanding.

Last Eight Words

These are the last eight words spoken by a business just before it begins to die while still attempting to produce an outdated product: "We have never done it that way before." These also become the last eight words spoken by followers of Jesus just before they enter a lifeless expression of faith: "I have never experienced God this way before."

These prohibitions—whether in a business, a church, or in our personal lives—will need to be confronted and dismantled if we are to move forward into new dimensions of revelation.

An example of this took place in the Jesus Movement of the 1960's. Pastors began to replace their suits and ties with shorts and sandals. They hung out with the beach culture of Southern California. Pastors told surfers about Jesus while floating on surfboards waiting for the next set of waves to arrive. An expression of the Church was birthed outside the walls of the religious establishment, and this led to a reformation in our thinking and our models of ministry.

God gave these brave young leaders such favor that some of the older leaders who led more traditional communities of faith gave their approval and support to these unconventional leaders. A movement was released that changed the landscape of Western Christianity.

We need to identify the barriers that stand in the way of reformation. The coming change will be truly miraculous. We have never walked this way before. Get ready! Winds of change are blowing across the face of the Earth, and waves of refreshment are approaching our shores. Start paddling! The wave you are about to catch will give you the ride of your life.

TWO

Experts of History

I am grateful for experts in any field of study, including history, but experts are not the gatekeepers of all wisdom. Understanding the past is not the only thing that moves the Church forward into new territory.

Faith sees what data and facts cannot see. Faith is the substance of things not yet seen, even by the experts. We move forward when we exercise our faith in the direction of what is not yet visible or knowable by natural means of evaluation or prediction. Experts follow behind to collect the evidence of an act of faith. They help us grow and learn and become informed. But history, data, and expert knowledge don't lead the way; those elements do not fuel faith.

The edge of expanding revelation is where reformation is birthed. There are no experts here because everything is untested and untraveled. In this place, new and previously unheard of instruction will come to spiritually hungry people—whether expert or novice. It is on these spiritual frontiers where previously hidden direction is revealed. The hall of faith described in Hebrews 11 is the historical record of this kind of person. We can learn from their example, but we aren't limited to it.

One day I had coffee with a pastor named Shawn. We had met earlier in a gathering of local church leaders. I asked to have coffee with him to get to know him. As we talked, it was obvious he had undergone some form of physical trauma. One side of his face had fallen like that of a stroke victim, and speaking from one side of his mouth was a challenge for him. I learned that some of his facial muscles had been immobilized due to nerve damage caused by a radical form of surgery.

Shawn told me his story. He had been having headaches, so he visited his doctor. He got terrible news: the doctor discovered a tumor that was pressing against his brain and spinal column. The pressure from the tumor could immediately stop his heart if it grew by even a single millimeter.

Shawn was scheduled for surgery. On the day of the operation, he was wheeled into surgery on a gurney. His wife, Christine, was walking alongside the gurney. Just before they reached the door leading to the surgery area, Christine stepped in front of the gurney, blocking it. She extended her hand toward her unresponsive husband and began to declare life and restoration.

In response to her declarations, Shawn's body began to twitch. The head nurse turned to Christine and said, "You are coming with us!" In an unprecedented act, the head nurse invited Christine to don the appropriate surgical gowns and be present to stand in prayer for her husband and the team conducting the delicate procedure. The surgery took eighteen hours.

Doctors had to remove part of Shawn's brain along with the tumor, which was the size of a tennis ball. After the surgery, Shawn was told he would not be able to perform the normal activities of life.

Yet here he was, sitting across the table from me. He pulled out his smartphone to show me an x-ray of his head. In the place where we have a large portion of brain tissue, my friend has a void filled with fluid.

I was talking with a miracle.

Shawn now drives his car, runs a successful business, and takes walks with his wife. God had another plan for Shawn, and He worked through his wife to declare a hope and new future that made no sense in the natural. But in that unseen future was healing and restoration, and those were released by an act of faith from Shawn's loving wife.

In moments of faith, there are no experts or rookies—only candidates for the miraculous. Gather all the expert advice you can and learn from others, but never forget that at some point you will get to exercise your faith and write a history the experts have not yet seen. It has been hidden in the heart of God, not in facts, figures, or a professional diagnosis.

In 1 Corinthians 2: 9-10, Paul quoted Isaiah to the church in Corinth:

> *"No eye has seen, no ear has heard,*
> *and no mind has imagined*
> *what God has prepared*
> *for those who love him."*

> *But it was to us that God revealed these things by his Spirit. For his Spirit searches out everything and shows us God's deep secrets.*

Prepare yourself to experience things no eye has seen, no ear has heard, and no mind has imagined. We are invited to live and believe the text of Ephesians 3:20:

> *Now all glory to God, who is able, through his mighty power at work within us, to accomplish infinitely more than we might ask or think.*

God is currently at work beyond what you could imagine or consider asking in your most ardent prayer. It is so fresh and simple that it will surprise you when it visits your family, your city, and nation.

Religious Koi Ponds

Recently, I returned home after a two-state, five-day road trip where I taught at several venues and reconnected with some wonderful churches. It was a solo trip. My wife, Jan, couldn't join me this time. Traveling alone is not my favorite method of travel, but God is always good and provides the kind of encounters with His presence that makes these trips well worth the effort.

The churches where I speak normally put me up in a hotel. It is refreshing to have your own private place when you are ministering in a variety of settings. On one part of this trip, my room was on the third floor of a hotel complex overlooking a beautiful courtyard surrounding a large pond filled with golden and white Koi. Some of the fish were over two feet in length. I stood at my window and watched them swim in circles. They swam hour after hour. Every time I went to my window, there they were still swimming in circles. I felt for these fish because that pond was the only reality they knew.

Those pond-bound fish are a sad metaphor for many of us; we can find ourselves trapped in theological ponds with a narrow and partial understanding of a much larger truth. We swim in circles within the confines of our limited level of thinking, believing that what we know is all there is to know. In these ponds, a larger God-reality seems impossible. But it isn't; we just haven't experienced it yet.

Everything begins to change when Jesus shows up and speaks of the larger river of His presence where He wants us to swim. The thought of being transferred, through a process of reformation, into a larger river can seem unnerving if not outright scary. Experiencing something new means leaving the familiar pond. Reformers are willing to plunge into new waters.

We were destined for a level of freedom in Jesus that a religious pond of narrow thinking and a short-sighted vision cannot provide. We have been created to swim unhindered in the river of God.

Paul said it so well when he addressed the church in Ephesus (Ephesians 3:18-19):

> *And may you have the power to understand, as all God's people should, how wide, how long, how high, and how deep his love is. May you experience the love of Christ, though it is too great to understand fully. Then you will be made complete with all the fullness of life and power that comes from God.*

The Lord will open our eyes and help us see where we have been swimming in confinement. We were not created to swim in circles. We are created to swim in the supernatural current of the river of God. That will require a level of faith that sees beyond the banks of our current pond. That Spirit-empowered sight was given to reformers in the past, and it is the same sight being given to reformers in this moment of history.

The Seven Mountains

Two alignments in the Church have been unfolding over the last several decades. The first is a renewed understanding of our mission in every sphere of culture. The second alignment has been a revisiting of the purpose of the five-fold gifts Jesus gave to the Church to equip each person for the work of ministry.

In 1975 two men, Bill Bright of Campus Crusade for Christ and Loren Cunningham of Youth with a Mission (YWAM) met in Colorado Springs. Each of them had—independently and while many miles apart—received the same word from the Lord. The word had to do with the spheres of cultural influence and the role of the Church in those spheres. The same word was also given to Francis Schaeffer at L'Abri in Switzerland.

Each of these three men began to train thousands of young men and women, who are now in places of leadership within the global Church.

During the Colorado Springs meeting, Bright and Cunningham identified the following seven spheres of cultural influence: government, religion, business, education, arts & entertainment, family, and media. Recently, writer-thinkers like Lance Wallnau and Johnny Enlow have unpacked and defined these spheres in greater detail. We now refer to them as the "Seven Mountains."

God is reminding the Church to reconsider the places of her mission. Our voice has an assignment on each of the Seven Mountains. Our willingness to allow the sound of Heaven to venture onto the slopes of these mountains will determine the level of cultural transformation in a time of reformation.

What would it look like to equip and commission the Church to go into every sphere of society and bring a positive influence for change? Some of us thought we were doing just that, but we were wrong. What if we have been camping on the summit of the mountain of religion, not understanding the greater opportunities that await us on the other six mountains of culture? Take an honest look at our culture. Who is influencing and reforming society? Right now, it is not the Church.

The Five-Fold Gifts

We need to rediscover the simple assignment of the five-fold ministry gifts given by Jesus and listed by Paul in Ephesians 4. Remember, these gifts are for training and equipping the Church for the work of ministry. The five-fold gifts are made up of apostles, prophets, evangelists, pastors, and teachers. To approach any of the Seven Mountains improperly equipped and without exposure to these gifts is a recipe for failure and irrelevance.

I don't want to over-define the five equipping gifts. Over-defining them might be part of our current problem. We may have mistakenly sought to understand these gifts with our logic and not our hearts. Knowing the heart of God is the wellspring from which all healthy understanding flows.

Recently, the desire to understand the function and purpose of these gifts has increased. I understand that desire, but in the process of deepening our understanding, we may have created an overly academic approach to their function.

Every gift, every talent, every one of the five equipping gifts, and every ministry in the Church must filter its function and interaction with people through our character and integrity. The development and release of the fruit of God's Spirit is where our most important understanding and definitions are discovered. If we are not producing the fruit of the Spirit, most of what we do in the name of God will become abusive, insensitive, and divisive. Our ministries will become as appealing as a bowl filled with bruised and rotting fruit.

If you want to learn how to function most effectively in your unique gift set, study the fruit of the Spirit before you study the gifts of the Spirit. You will need more character than you need gifting because your character is what will carry your gift over the long haul. This will enlarge the ability of the Church to impact culture. Paul wrote in Ephesians 4:13 that the ministry of the equipping gifts would continue...

> *...until we all come to such unity in our faith and knowledge of God's Son that we will be mature in the Lord, measuring up to the full and complete standard of Christ.*

The Scripture implies that without these five equipping gifts—without their example and instruction—the Church cannot measure up to the full and complete standard of Christ. In other words, we need these gifts to help us understand and experience a practical oneness in our faith and the fullness of what it means to know Jesus. That is a life-long process, one that will never end as long as you and I live on planet Earth.

The One-Size-Fits-All Glove of Ministry

When I began to pastor my first church almost forty years ago, we had a "one-size-glove-fits-all" approach to ministry. If you were called to lead in a traditional church setting, you had one glove in which to insert your gift. That glove was labeled "pastor." If your predominant equipping gift was that of pastor, then there was no problem. But if you were a teacher or an evangelist, the fit was less comfortable. If your gift was apostle or a prophet, the fit was even more difficult.

Various ministries have risen in recent years to help release people into their unique calling. Many people in the Church have thrived in missions work overseas, where the equipping gifts flourished with less restriction. This was true for me when we were sent overseas as missionaries. In that context, I was much more in my element.

Over the years, I have taken several gift assessment tests. Pastor was usually the lowest return in my test results. Prophet was at the top followed by apostle, teacher, evangelist, and finally, pastor. My wife, Jan, has the pastoral gift. It is her nature, gift, and calling. That is why I could survive inside the ill-fitting glove of pastoral ministry. We were a well-balanced team. Eighteen years ago, Jan and I returned to the United States from missions to pastor our third church. We settled back into the only glove available to us at the time, slipping our hands back into the one-size-fits-all glove of pastor.

A few years ago, I asked the Lord to help me understand why I had spent all those years in pastoral assignments when that was not my primary calling. He showed me that my time as a pastor helped me learn how to create healthy environments in each setting where the Lord called me to serve. Nothing is ever wasted with God, even what appears to be a mismatch of our gift and assignment.

In all my years of ministry, I was able to experience just about every conflict and struggle one can go through. I can honestly say to a struggling leader, "I understand," because I do. Now, as a spiritual father, I can help them see how to move forward when faced with what appears to be insurmountable obstacles. I can be a mentoring presence and speak prophetic words of encouragement that release an alignment to God's heart and calling.

In the middle of this learning curve, I knew the Church needed all the equipping gifts, but I was not sure how to facilitate their release. In the process of personal discovery of my passions and contribution, I saw that I was not a misfit in the local church setting. I simply needed to expand my understanding of my calling and my placement in the living organism called the Church. I also learned that when we are led by the Spirit we can function in any of the gifts—regardless of whether one or another is our predominant gift. This was true in all my years of serving in pastoral ministry when that was not my primary gift.

As a pastor, I wasn't supposed to do all the work of the ministry. My assignment was to train and release others in their unique gifts. In the last local church we pastored, we were there long enough to develop a leadership team that worked as a unit, making decisions together. I never wanted to be a dictatorial presence. Three years ago, I handed over my pastoral assignment to this team who had shared in the care of our faith community.

This process of equipping our church family also included gifts from outside our local team. As it was in the Early Church, we received visiting leaders across the five-fold spectrum who brought us needed encouragement and alignment. Some of these came from ministry settings very different from ours. We also had equipping gifts on our leadership teams who worked in our community but not as part of our paid staff. These people helped us to see outside the walls of our church and into the heart of our city.

If you are struggling with the glove dilemma you have two options. You can find a place where the fit of your unique glove awaits your gift, or you can start from where you currently find yourself and learn a new reality. Allow yourself to be taught, and then teach those in your care what it means to place your hand into the right glove.

God has a unique glove for each of us to wear. Your glove may not be one of the five equipping gifts. It might be hospitality or miracles or administration. Whatever glove fits your hand, put it on and wear it with confidence.

The Five-Fold Blueprint

Early in my ministry, the idea of the five equipping gifts was a bit foreign to me. I could understand the pastor and teacher gift, and even an occasional visit from a traveling evangelist for a mid-week service. Apostles and prophets were unfamiliar roles to me.

Some of the teaching regarding these gifts has grown complicated and professional. This has unintentionally distanced emerging generations from the purpose and valuable place these gifts are meant to have in all spheres of culture.

I have come to a simple understanding of these five gifts and their functions. It may not be perfect but it works for me. Here's how I see them:

- APOSTLES receive Heaven's blueprint
- PROPHETS announce the blueprint
- EVANGELISTS recruit for the blueprint
- PASTORS create environments where the blueprint can grow and thrive
- TEACHERS expand and teach in detail each element of the blueprint

Apostles receive Heaven's blueprint of God's preferred future. These blueprints are God's plans for cultural transformation and Kingdom expansion. Prophets confirm and proclaim God's plans, becoming the voice for the blueprint. Evangelists tell seekers about the message of the blueprint and the wonderful things God has done and will do if they choose to follow the Lord. Pastors create a place of communion and honor where the plans of God can grow and flourish in a safe environment. Teachers expand and explain each detail of the truths contained in the blueprint; like an engineer, they create a detailed schematic drawing of a complex machine to explain each part and its relationship to the whole in understandable detail and terminology.

These definitions are not limited to the mountain of religion or to the professional clergy. They are intended to function in fullness on all of the Seven Mountains and within every profession.

The Five Equipping Gifts Produce Maturity

We need the five equipping gifts to become mature in our faith, fully developed in Jesus Christ.

To be mature means we are not shaken every time we face a challenge. Paul describes immaturity in Ephesians 4:14:

> *Then we will no longer be immature like children. We won't be tossed and blown about by every wind of new teaching. We will not be influenced when people try to trick us with lies so clever they sound like the truth.*

In the verse before this, Ephesians 4:13, the word Paul used to describe maturity can be translated as "ripe." The obvious reference would be to the ripeness of fruit. Ripeness is that perfect moment when all the contributing elements of nature come together to produce a piece of fruit in a state of sweet maturity. To bite into a fully ripened fruit and experience its sweet flavor is the reason why a farmer planted his seeds in the first place.

As a young boy in California, I picked fruit during the summers. I worked for Mr. Dardanelli, who owned the orchard across the street from my home. Mr. Dardanelli was an Italian-American who kindly helped some of us neighborhood boys discover the value of work. I grew up in the Silicon Valley. It was much different from what it is today. When I was a boy, it was a valley filled with orchards as far as the eye could see. In the springtime, when the white petals of the blossoms fell from the fruit trees, it was like snowfall.

On many summer mornings, my brother and I, along with some of our friends, would hop in the back of Mr. Dardanelli's 1949 Chevy pickup truck and ride out into an apricot orchard. Each of us wore the uniform of boys in the 1950's and early 1960's: a white t-shirt, blue jeans, and black high-top tennis shoes.

Mr. Dardanelli knew the exact time to pick buckets full of perfectly ripe apricots. On one of those summer mornings, I climbed to the top of my ladder with a bucket in hand. At the top of the tallest branch hung a perfect apricot. It was large and full of color with a mist of morning dew moistening its skin. I reached up and picked the fruit. I knew I was harvesting the apricot at the ideal moment. It could not get any better. A day later it would not be this good.

When I held the apricot in my hand, I knew it was destined for my hungry stomach. As I bit into its sweet flesh, a burst of flavor filled my mouth. It was the perfect apricot picked on the perfect morning on one of the most beautiful of all California mornings. I still remember that day in vivid detail.

This is the essence of what maturity should be like. The equipping gifts are used to train us up to a place of maturity where the fruit of the Spirit is ripened in us. At that time, we will have been fully developed in the life and abundance of Jesus Christ. We will emanate His sweetness and the fragrance of the Spirit, like that of a perfect apricot picked at the peak of its maturity.

Going Round the Mountain

You have heard the phrase, "Going around the mountain again." This phrase is normally couched in negative tones. That negative reality can exist if we are unwilling to be led by the Lord. But there is another way to understand that phrase.

In Psalm 23, David writes about God leading us to green pastures and guiding us along right paths. Those who study the culture of ancient Israel and understand the terrain know that these paths can circle up the mountain toward the summit.

David wrote this Psalm about tending his father's sheep. It was common practice for shepherds to move their herds up and around a mountain in a circling fashion.

We don't arrive at the top of any mountain without some form of journey. From a Kingdom perspective, these circular pathways are not negative. Going around the mountain again means we just gained more altitude. When we look back to our starting point, we see how far we have climbed.

These treks around the mountain are actually part of our maturing process, helping us gain a progressively higher dimension of calling and revelation. As we mature, we are less likely to throw spiritual and emotional temper tantrums when faced with uncertain times and uncomfortable challenges. As we mature, we no longer look back on the ascent with regret. We come to understand that Jesus is always leading us to something higher, just like David when he cared for his father's flock.

The Result of a Five-Fold Ministry

The apostles, prophets, evangelists, pastors, and teachers equip us to do the work of ministry. So, what *is* the work of ministry we are being equipped to do?

I would guess that most of us think this equipping is done to enable people to run local churches, denominations, or other ministries. The five-fold can include that, but to limit our understanding to the mountain of religion at the expense of the other six mountains would be to limit the scope of the Church's impact on Earth.

Paul revealed the result of this equipping in Ephesians. Notice two important words: *then* and *instead*:

> **Then**, *we will no longer be immature like children. We won't be tossed and blown about by every wind of new teaching. We will not be influenced when people try to trick us with lies so clever they sound like the truth.* **Instead**, *we will speak the truth in love, growing in every way more and more like Christ, who is the head of his body, the church* (Ephesians 4:14-15, emphasis mine).

Here is a primary concept I hope to convey in this book: *speaking the truth in love is the evidence that we have been equipped and matured as believers.* It is the evidence that we are experiencing the fullness of what it means to know Jesus.

We will hear the sound of reformation when the voice of a matured Church becomes one with the unique frequency of God's love expressed on the mountains of culture. When this begins to take place, the truth of God's limitless, all-consuming love will be heard with wonder and amazement in every sphere of society.

Over the years, I have seen unusual displays of maturity—and not always in the way I would expect. I recall a time when a family I knew was navigating an especially challenging season. The father, mother, and their teenage daughter met with me in an attempt to reconcile.

I had listened to the parents share their struggle but felt something was amiss. I then asked the daughter to share her side of the story. It did not take long for me to realize it was the daughter who was the mature person in this family drama.

The parents were distant from fellowship and community. They were not involved in any setting where they were being challenged to grow spiritually. The daughter was proactive in her desire to follow Jesus. She was being trained and discipled in youth ministry, and she was establishing close connections with our community. She was maturing spiritually.

I shared with the family my understanding of the process of maturity for each follower of Jesus. I said it was not chronological time that promised maturity. It was our willingness to allow God to form our thinking and responses to life.

These parents came to my office thinking I would demand their daughter align with their unhealthy thinking. Without demeaning the parents, I helped them see the larger picture. Never in our meeting did the daughter dishonor her parents. With her words and her actions, she expressed a mature love.

What if all the complicated definitions of a five-fold ministry are really about a function—not a style or system? What if these gifts of the Holy Spirit, with their multiple expressions, actually came down to one simple thing: helping equip and train us to know how to speak the truth in love in our unique life-assignment on any of the Seven Mountains of culture? I'd like to suggest it is that simple.

Oneness

Everything pertaining to life flows from Jesus. He is the anointing head of His body, the Church. Our ministries, our calling, and our destiny all flow from Him.

His *body*, the Church, has been formed in His image. Paul writes in Ephesians 4:16:

> *He makes the whole body fit together perfectly. As each part does its own special work, it helps the other parts grow, so that the whole body is healthy and growing and full of love.*

Another way to describe a body *fit together perfectly* is *compacted*. In all of the diversity of the Church, Jesus has the uncanny ability to be able to fit us tightly together—to compact us in love into a single unit while we still maintain our uniqueness. In this compacting, nothing is crushed. If we allow the heart of God to empower our fellowship instead of demanding that our points of division and separation must first come together, we will fit together with Him and with each other in perfect union.

Oneness is a powerful concept. Jesus said that He and the Father are one. Jesus said we are one with Him. Scripture tells us that one faith was delivered to the Church. Jesus told his early disciples the world would believe in Him when they see our oneness. Oneness is paramount in God's Kingdom.

The marriage of a man and woman is a great expression of oneness. No other relationship on Earth expresses the kind of oneness experienced by a husband and wife. You cannot have this depth of oneness with your best friend, your children, or any other close relationship. A marriage creates a relationship where two complete and unique individuals are joined together to become one. Before their marriage, while they were single, they were complete. After their marriage, these two, complete people became one. Have you noticed the math of God seems to always add up to one? In God's Kingdom, one plus one equals one.

When Jan and I were married forty-four years ago, we were two kids who knew little about life or love. We learned along the way. Forgiveness was always our way forward. It still is to this day.

Jan is very different from me. She works with great detail on the micro scale. I am the opposite. I work quickly on the macro scale. For example, after I wrote this book, Jan read the first draft because she can see things no one else can see. We have learned how to mature together in our oneness. In my writing, she keeps me vulnerable and precise. Sometimes it's a real struggle when you think you have something nailed down only to have the other half of your oneness show you a completely different perspective.

As another example, when we have a house-painting project, Jan knows where to assign my painting "talent." I am given the large, quick swathes to paint with a roller. Jan is an expert at cutting in the fine lines at transition points and around the molding of doors and windows. We know each other's uniqueness, and we have learned how to work together.

We are at the place in our relationship where I no longer know where I end and Jan begins or vice versa. Our oneness has compacted us together until we are one. This compacting is a unity only God can create. He brings together very different people and makes them one if they are willing to be pressed together in love. As we mature, we continually learn how to work together in our diversity.

The Purpose of Love

A pastor named Jerry Cook deeply impacted my life—and the lives of thousands of others. I got to know Jerry when he pastored Easthill Church in Gresham, Oregon. In the 1970's, when so many of us were trying to find our way through a confusing and complicated season in our national history, Jerry wrote the seminal book, *Love, Acceptance, and Forgiveness.*

Jerry helped many of us discover—and in some cases rediscover—the simplicity of our mission as the Church. Some of the most foundational aspects of life in the Spirit had been buried under the busyness of ministry and the unhealthy expectations of other people. Jerry also helped the Charismatic and Pentecostal segments of the Church engage their intellect and learn how to think, not just emote.

With any new thing God does, there will be a certain amount of mystery and the mystical. Any new revelation about God and how He works can be strangely wonderful. Heaven's perspective cannot be fully grasped by the natural mind and can sound or look foolish if we are not willing to see an expression of our faith outside the box of our current level of experience.

During that season, I sat in a meeting of pastors with Jerry. He was asked to define love. He said, "Love is seeking the highest good for another person." When I heard those words, they became permanently tattooed in my mind. I have carried that definition of love ever since.

Seeking the highest good for another person will involve speaking the truth in love at all costs. It has to be expressed in word or deed. It must be truth, and it must be expressed in love, or it will have no lasting effect. This is not an easy assignment to actually carry out. It is the responsibility of the five equipping gifts to prepare us to be able to experience and express God's truth in love.

Whenever truth and love are released, the creativity of God is also released, and reformation is soon to follow.

Force or Field

One of the concepts Jerry Cook presented in his book was the idea of the Church being either a force or a field. Among other things, this understanding helped us see how local churches were represented in culture and how to train and send out people into the various spheres of culture.

The Church as a field means that just about everything is centralized around the church facility and programs. We come to a building to be the Church. We invite people to our facility to experience the love of God. This model greatly reduces the ability of the Church to have significant impact on the mountains of culture.

On the other hand, the Church as a force is not secluded within protective walls. It is a community trained to live out its message of truth, equipped to go out in love onto every mountain of culture.

Jerry Cook was prophetic about this current moment in our history. A church trained and released by the five equipping gifts is a force. This force will gather together in community to learn and grow, and then it will walk out into the streets of its city to represent God's message of love, acceptance, and forgiveness. Followers of Jesus are the most significant force for change on the face of the Earth. We just need to be awakened to that possibility.

A Kingdom Mindset

Jesus told His first disciples what would come after their experience on the Day of Pentecost:

> *But you will receive power when the Holy Spirit comes upon you. And you will be my witnesses, telling people about me everywhere — in Jerusalem, throughout Judea, in Samaria, and to the ends of the earth* (Acts 1:8, emphasis mine).

The operative word is *everywhere.*

When Jesus used the word *witnesses,* He was not limiting the ability to bring a witness to the professionally labeled ministries that have historically operated on the mountain of religion. He was addressing something much larger.

The training and sending out of traditional pastors, teachers, and evangelists will continue, but it will also expand to include the training and sending out of politicians, sanitation workers, CEOs, teachers, sculptors, newscasters, Wal-Mart greeters, and a million other job titles that will add to our missionary pool. The mission of the Church will no longer be limited by the activities taking place on the mountain of religion.

Shortly after Pentecost, the Early Church gathered in increasing numbers at Solomon's Colonnade until persecution scattered them. Jesus never intended for His followers to just gather in one place and focus inwardly. Our calling is always outward. A variety of reasons exist for our dispersion. In this time of reformation, dissatisfaction with the status quo is behind some of the dispersion away from the existing model of Church as we know it.

On the road to Damascus, Jesus encountered a raging Pharisee who lived his life on the mountain of religion. It was a mountain protected and isolated from the other realms of culture. That angry and isolated man would later become known as the Apostle Paul.

Paul traveled to many regions of the known world because of his specific, apostolic calling. Yet, for a season he worked in a small, tent-making business with his friends, Aquila and Priscilla. Paul never missed a beat. He didn't have to get a hall pass to leave the mountain of religion to enter the mountain of business. A Kingdom mindset has fluidity and freedom.

Many of us have climbed the familiar mountains of religion and family, but now God is asking us to consider the other unscaled mountains of culture.

Shouting at People

It is too easy for the Church to remain isolated and to shout our displeasure at the other cultural mountains where people look and sound different from us. If we are not careful, we can let our differing mindsets and values create a negative and hostile representation of the Gospel instead of one that sounds like the Good News of Jesus Christ. We need to learn how to make a different sound.

The next wave of missionaries is not necessarily studying in our Bible colleges and seminaries. They are in the marketplace of their professions. They are learning the languages of their chosen professions while speaking with the welcoming sound of love. This expression of love does not compromise core beliefs; it is the same heart expressed by Paul when he talked to the Athenians about the statue dedicated to an Unknown God. Love gives our voice a platform from which to communicate the heart of God.

Some of these new missionaries are studying political science in state-run universities. Their influence on the mountain of government will come from investing the time needed to learn the systems and language of that mountain. Others are apprenticing to become electricians. Others are studying preschool education in community colleges, learning how to operate a preschool. The list of possibilities is as large as our imaginations and a culture's needs. All of these new missionaries will have one thing in common: they are educating themselves in their fields. They are creating platforms from where they can offer Kingdom solutions to complex problems.

Some followers of Jesus have felt it is their religious

duty to call out the evil they see in the music industry. They think the sound of their opposition will bring change. It never has and never will. Shouting at people in disgusted tones does not bring transformation; you might make a lot of noise but not many friends These misguided confrontations only create a wider divide and never build a platform for communication. We can do so much better.

There are groups of creative musicians within the Church waiting for someone to give them a green light to step off the mountain of religion and journey onto the mountain of arts & entertainment, crossing the chasm of separation between the Church and the music industry. These men and women do not feel called to express their gift and their musical talents only from a sanctuary platform on Sunday morning. The sound of their music has an assignment to be heard on a different mountain.

Why is a traditionally defined pastor considered a more noble calling than that of a foreman on a framing crew who cares for his coworkers on the construction site? Is the mission of a Home Depot employee who evangelizes her fellow workers in the break room any less significant than a traveling evangelist with a website? We could keep asking these questions using every job title on Earth and still come away with the same answer: no!

Somehow we have thought that staying on the mountains of religion and family was our safe place. From that place, we have voiced displeasure but not solutions. As a result, we have not allowed God to help us explore creative environments where the love of God—not our displeasure—can be shared. The divide between the sacred and what we perceive as secular will be bridged in the coming reformation because the future effectiveness of the Church requires it.

The Four Questions

When I pastored local churches, I asked each of our leaders four questions during our quarterly planning meetings. These questions were to discover any unhealthy trends we needed to correct to keep us on track with our vision, mission, and values. Here are the four questions:

1. What do we like about what we are doing?
2. What do we not like about what we are doing"
3. What do we want to keep?
4. What do we want to get rid of?

In an honest environment where questions are not a threat but part of a healthy process, these four questions can save a lot of wasted time, energy, and disappointment. We continued to ask these questions over the years. It became an anticipated exercise, because this practice kept us fresh and unassuming. Inquiring of the Lord on a regular basis kept us in the current flow of the Spirit. What we planned one year might or might not be what we were supposed to do the following year. Often, we would go for two or more years, and then something would change. That way we would not hold on to pet projects just because they had become tradition. As we continued to ask the four questions, we became more agile, simple, and more in tune to the leading of the Spirit.

Some of the things that were flushed out over the years were my bright and energetic ideas that I either suggested at the wrong time or that were not from God at all but rather from my enthusiasm. Be careful asking these kinds of questions with free and fearless people. It can change your world, and that is the real intention of the questions. These four questions, along with similar ones, are being asked in this time of shifting within the Church.

What would happen if you sat down with some trusted friends and asked these four questions about everything—even the beliefs you inherited but never studied in light of Scripture, historical context, and experience?

In the churches I pastored, we inherited some assumptions. Those assumptions did not help us—they required too much time and energy to maintain. We can continue propping up these unchallenged assumptions long enough for the next generation to come along and pick up the same burden, or we can ask tough questions.

I talk with a lot of young leaders. They don't want what we have carried in the past. They want something different. They want simple and authentic. Ask the hard questions, and you will be better able to hand off a healthy inheritance to the generation that follows.

What would happen if you gathered with a group of people who carried an apostolic vision for the city where you serve? What kind of blueprint would God give you to re-envision your city? How would you prepare people to lay the groundwork? What kind of answers would you have to the four questions? The answers to all of these questions will prepare you to move with the Spirit into a season of reformation.

Eating the Grapes of God's Goodness

Jan and I live in an historic mining town in Southern Oregon. One winter day as we walked into town, we came across piles of grapes on the sidewalk. I stopped and looked up to see a large grape vine growing overhead. A balcony overhangs the sidewalk there and has become a trellis for the vine. Up from a hole in the cement sidewalk, a very old grape vine climbs and has intertwined its vine into the structure of the balcony.

It was almost Christmas. To my surprise, I saw many large clusters of grapes still hanging on the leafless vine. This is a wine-growing region. Grapes do well in our mild climate. Still, the harvest of wine grapes had been over several months prior. It was now December. These grapes seemed out of season. As I started to take a photo of them, the Lord began to download a word.

He told me, "This is a time for the release of forgotten fruit from a previous season. This fruit has hung in suspension over you for an appointed release at this time. My seasons are not subject to the cycles of growth and harvest in the natural realm. Fruit will fall on your pathway, out of season, as a surprise blessing. You think the time of fruitfulness has passed, but I have always had a plan in place to release continual fruitfulness in every season. Its release has been waiting for my command. I have now given the command for supernatural fruit to fall on your life. I love to surprise you with my goodness. I have caused this sweet fruit to remain on the vine for this time of release. This will be my gift for you. I want to let you know I have not forgotten."

I know those words were not just for me. They apply to all of us who follow Jesus. We will harvest clusters of God's goodness and give them to the world as a blessing. The recipients will taste the sweetness of a good God in times and places where they thought the goodness and sweetness of God was not possible.

Does what we give to the world taste sweet and release the goodness of God? If not, we need to find out why and begin planting a new vineyard.

The arrival of this new fruit will take place in the most unusual and unexpected places, like it did the day I saw grapes on the sidewalk. The fruit of the seeds of reformation is beginning to drop onto the sidewalk of the Church. It is time to taste its sweetness and release its goodness everywhere we turn.

THREE

Theological Bounce Houses

One day as I was driving home, I saw one of those large, colorful bounce houses—those inflatable rubber structures brought to life by a motorized air pump. Kids jump and bounce around in them at birthday parties.

The image remained with me throughout the day, and that evening, the Lord gave me further understanding of it. I saw the Lord walking over and pulling the plug to the air pump. The bounce house slowly deflated until it lay on the ground in an unrecognizable pile of colorful plastic. People started crawling out from beneath the deflated bounce house with shocked looks on their faces.

I asked the Lord what this meant, and immediately, He took me back to the image. The people who crawled out from beneath the deflated bounce house had been transformed. Gravity no longer inhibited them. They began to bounce with each new step. They looked like astronauts jumping on the moon taking exaggerated leaps of faith; they were flying ahead in large, bouncing strides of Kingdom advancement.

The Lord said, "I am deflating religious structures that have falsely promised life." I understood His words to mean He was coming after the structures of our belief systems, our methods, and even our preferred styles of worship. These inflated structures have kept us isolated—unable to engage the culture in a significant way. They require too much expense and too much energy to keep inflated. They are overly complex and keep us in a limited place of increasing irrelevance.

God is pulling the plug on what we have used to keep us falsely inflated. Much of what will be deflated in the coming reformation will be the complicated religious structures that have replaced the sweet simplicity of Jesus Christ. God is deflating them because they will not be able carry us into the future He has prepared for us. When the collapse takes place, people will crawl out from under the weight of what no longer works, ready to receive a fresh breath of God's Spirit.

As the image of the bounce house came to an end, I saw thousands upon thousands of us bouncing to the tops of each of the Seven Mountains. When we landed on these summits, we set foot at altitudes of influence we previously thought unreachable.

Confess, Repent, Move

When we think of the words, "confess" and "repent," we tend to think of sin. While these words can refer to sin, they also have a broader meaning.

The word "confess" actually means to agree. When we confess our sins, we are agreeing with God that what is taking place in our life is not His intended best for us. The word "repent" means to change the way we think. For years, I was taught that repentance meant changing my behavior. More accurately, repentance is first changing my thinking, which will then change my behavior.

When we talk of a reformation in the Church, we must first agree with God that something is missing; something is not adding up or is even terribly wrong. That confession sets us up to have our thinking adjusted and aligned with God's heart. When we agree with God and let Him change how we think, we can then express His message and mission with clarity and simplicity. That's how the Kingdom moves forward.

Shift, Alignment, & the Suddenly of God

In each new move of God, small or large, three things take place in a chain of events: a shift, an alignment, and a "suddenly." Over the last several years, everywhere I turn I hear people saying, "there is a shift taking place." Jan and I have been saying the same thing, and we have been seeing it personally and in the larger Church. We are in the middle of a major shift.

A shift first begins in our spirit with the recognition of our own narrow and restricted way of thinking. Once that limited or even false belief is identified, God will begin the process of turning us in a new direction. The new direction will bring an alignment to a new compass heading. Those alignments point toward the direction where the next "suddenly" of God has been assigned to appear.

The first disciples experienced a tremendous shift when Jesus was crucified. It dismantled the reality they had known for three years. Their response to the shift was to fearfully lock themselves in the Upper Room. In a short while, they would be aligned with the direction of two approaching suddenlies: a supernatural visitation of the resurrected Lord and the outpouring of the Spirit on the Day of Pentecost.

When we talk about a suddenly of God, we tend to think of large events like the Day of Pentecost or a major revival. The Book of Acts was recorded over the course of forty years. Among the significant encounters recorded in Acts, people lived normal, everyday lives.

The Early Church also processed and matured through periods of waiting and trusting and hoping. In the waiting, they struggled with discouragement and feelings of weakness just like we do today—2,000 years removed from their experience. This is why when Paul visited churches, he strengthened and encouraged them. Why did Paul need to do this? Because normal people will have times of discouragement and moments when they feel too weak to go on with life. We need people like Paul to come and remind us of who we are and the God who walks with us. This is one of the most critical tasks of a reformer. The Church moves forward with hope, not judgment.

Flying Into New Opportunities

I mentioned earlier that I worked as a flight instructor. That job supplemented my income as a pastor when our family lived in a small town in Montana in the 1980's. It was also a way for me to escape the feeling of being trapped in a mountain valley during the long, frigid Montana winters.

When I became a flight instructor, I had no idea that God was setting me up to encounter people I would never have met had I not learned to fly and teach flying.

With my instructor rating, I was able to perform the flight checks required by the FAA for pilots to remain current and legal. Business people who owned aircraft contracted with me to provide these check rides. I began to build relationships with some of the most influential people in our small town. Because I was now a fixture in their lives, I was present when they needed counsel or when a memorial service or a marriage took place and they needed someone to officiate.

Some of these encounters became spiritual suddenlies where God made Himself known in a personal way. My ability to fly and train others had become an open door of influence I would never have imagined.

My feelings of being trapped were not just about the cold, snowbound winters or the remoteness of my town. My flying experience gave me a perspective beyond the four walls of a church building. I was no longer constrained by the restrictions associated with the traditional role of a pastor in a local church. I was now part of my community.

Discern the stirrings in your heart. A shift might be taking place. If it is a shifting stirred by God's Spirit, it will lead you to an alignment that will point you in the direction of a suddenly of God. Whether it is a sudden work of God or an unfolding reformation, He uses both methods to deliver us to destinations we never thought possible.

Fear and Fearful People

What we don't know of God can scare us. We can get complacent with what we know of Him and think it is sufficient. It's not. There are elements of the faith long ago delivered to the Church that we are still unpacking. When these elements emerge, they can seem like strange and unfamiliar doctrines when in reality they have been forgotten, misunderstood, or abandoned over time.

I remember the release of the film, *The Da Vinci Code*. Jan and I enjoyed the movie as entertainment. It was a work of fiction; it neither formed nor challenged our faith.

Not long after we saw the film, I was in a local bookstore when a woman from our church approached me. She had a very concerned look on her face. She said, "Pastor, some of my friends are having their faith challenged by the movie. What should I do?" I said in response, "Ask them what their faith is built upon." That one comment erased the concern from her face. The woman said, "Thank you for the reminder."

Change will challenge what we believe, and it will expose our fear. The Early Church fathers had a wise saying: "In the essentials unity; in the non-essentials liberty; in all things, love." Those who have the essentials of faith nailed down will be the ones who will navigate a time of reformation with less personal trauma and unbridled emotion.

Dropping the Box

One day, as I made my way home after a morning of errands and appointments, I noticed a car pulling out in front of me with an unsecured box on its roof. The driver had probably set it there while doing something else and then forgot it when he drove off. As the car made a turn onto the roadway, the box fell off. I stopped to pick it up and hoped to catch the driver, but he drove away before I could get his attention.

At first I thought I would go to our local post office and leave the package, since it had an address attached. Then I noticed the return address was only a few blocks away, so I drove there, hoping to find the owner. I knocked on the door, but no one answered, so I left the box on the front porch.

Driving away, I felt a sense of joy. I also felt the heart of God for us. How many times have we driven off to our next appointment, busy with the demands of the day, and lost something along the way, like sensitivity to the needs of other people or a sense of peace. The complicated lives we have created within the luxury and freedom of Western culture are not what Jesus originally intended.

God has a reformation process planned that will return to us our lost simplicity and a resulting peace. Like the person driving off without his box, at some point we notice that we have lost something we once valued. Reformation is the opportunity to get back our boxes.

Imagine the feelings of the person who drove around town and finally realized their package was missing. Contrast that to the joy of arriving home later in the day and seeing the lost package waiting on the porch. God has planned similar restoration for many of us in the coming reformation. We will rediscover lost simplicity. Joy will greet us on our return home—a return to a simpler calling, and a return to find what we had lost waiting for us on the porch of our life.

When I returned the box, I left a short note explaining what happened without leaving my name. I ended the note with the words, "God Bless you!" When God returns lost things, He blesses the recipient not only with the return of what was lost, but with the joy that comes when we know He is watching over us.

Chaos Theory

As I look across our global culture, I see more chaos than order. Growing up in the United States, I always carried a sense of optimism. Having lived and traveled in parts of the world held back by injustice, I see the United States—with all our flaws and imperfections—as a beacon of hope to the world.

On the brink of reformation, we have felt a shaking here at home and around the world. Some people feel overwhelmed by the tremors of change and the resulting chaos. They have thrown up their hands and given up trying to understand why so much is shifting.

When I was a young cop, I was assigned to a unit called the Organized Crime and Criminal Information Section, or OCCIS. There were ten of us undercover officers on the team. We altered our appearance to blend in with the clientele we pursued. We had fake IDs and cars registered to a dummy corporation, including a false-front office with an undercover secretary. We were untraceable.

In OCCIS, our assignment was to look for patterns in criminal organizations and use those patterns to uncover hidden illegal activity. Some of those same techniques are being used today to discover the perpetrators of human trafficking.

As part of my training, I was sent to a data collection class. It was a two-week training intensive held in Sacramento, California. One of our instructors was a chain-smoking, ex-CIA officer. His field of expertise was mathematics. Using math, statistics, and graphing techniques, he could determine if a crime was taking place in a business. He would stake out a restaurant for a week with a menu in hand. By measuring the foot traffic, he could determine if a money laundering operation was in play by comparing the data he compiled with the tax returns the business filed. He helped us see how to find crime patterns in a sea of data not obvious to a casual observer.

In matters of the Spirit, you have been given the ability to see patterns in the chaos of culture and within the Church. Don't become overwhelmed by the pace of life or the unpleasant events taking place. You have not been left in the dark. You have been given the gift of discernment.

The gift of discernment remains an untapped resource because it is held captive to the obvious. The prophetic assignment of the Church is to see beyond the obvious. As a follower of Jesus, you have been given the ability to view every situation with the penetrating insight of the Spirit. Just like the ex-CIA analyst helped me see how an innocent-looking restaurant in a quiet neighborhood was actually a money-laundering operation for organized crime, you are in training to discern truth from lies in spiritual matters. You have been given the Spirit-empowered ability to see through a veil of what appears normal and everyday and to uncover what is really taking place.

To the discerning observer, it is evident the Church is no longer impacting our culture in a significant way. There are some pockets of hope, but overall we need a fresh move of God's Spirit to shift us and realign us. We have become insular and isolated from culture. We defend that position with religious reasoning.

There is hope. People are beginning to ask the right questions, and those questions are creating the shift we are currently experiencing. Don't let your insight and your voice be robbed of its impact by throwing up your hands in disgust or despair and walking away. Just like the Early Church, you have been placed in your surrounding culture for a reason: to bring light into dark places. To do this you must be able to see what is hidden from the casual observer.

The discovery of deception is part of God's redemptive process. He wants to shine His light of truth and love into hidden places to expose and dismantle every evil enterprise. This is not exposure for the purpose of finding fault; it is the exposure of hell's laundering scheme that has individuals and entire cultures settling for something less than God's best.

FOUR

Kingdom Cartographers

Recently, I heard the Lord say, "I am redrawing the borders." As I continued to listen, He said, "I am redrawing the borders of My Church to reveal your spiritual authority and new spheres of influence. The resulting realignment is not limited to the national borderlines on your maps. These lines of authority are only seen in the spiritual realm." The Lord went on to say, "Ask Me for the discernment needed to see what I am doing. With this expansion will come the release of the apostolic teams I will use to establish My reign within these newly formed jurisdictions."

When Jan and I lived in Europe, I read and studied the history of the nations on the European continent. The borders we see on our current maps were not always there. They have shifted many times over the last thousand years. The same is true for other regions of the world. Nations and empires were constantly redefined and redrawn as the result of wars and alliances formed by royal marriage and commerce.

God's map is drawn differently. Underneath the migrating borders of each nation there exists a spiritual map drawn by God that reveals a deeper reality. That map is the one God wants us to use to direct our effort and energy.

Whenever I drive or fly into a new region, I always pray when I cross a defining border. Even a sign announcing a new county line or city limits prompts me to pray for wisdom and discernment to see beneath the natural border in order to understand what is taking place in the realm of the Spirit.

The Lord was telling me that I needed discernment to see spiritual lines of definition regardless of natural borders. I needed to see His intentions as well as the real conflict that is often hidden. Realignment in the spiritual realm precedes realignment in the natural realm.

Discern these new borders with expansion in mind. When Luke wrote Acts 1:6-8, he shared the words of Jesus addressing that expansion:

> *So when the apostles were with Jesus, they kept asking him, "Lord, has the time come for you to free Israel and restore our kingdom?" He replied, "The Father alone has the authority to set those dates and times, and they are not for you to know. But you will receive power when the Holy Spirit comes upon you. And you will be my witnesses, telling people about me everywhere—In Jerusalem, throughout Judea, in Samaria, and to the ends of the earth."*

The disciples initially saw the Kingdom confined to a single area defined by existing and familiar borders. Jesus was telling His disciples that after the Day of Pentecost, everything would change. The Holy Spirit would have them step through the restraints of existing national borders and cultural prohibitions to move into new territory. While in Jerusalem, the disciples were asked to look to the uttermost parts of the Earth as their ultimate destination. Their understanding opened and they moved under the direction and definition of God's unseen Kingdom map.

Jesus told the disciples that those who could see what they were seeing and hear what they were hearing were blessed:

"Blessed are the eyes that see what you have seen. I tell you, many prophets and kings longed to see what you see, but they didn't see it. And they longed to hear what you hear, but they didn't hear it" (Luke 10:23b-24).

Blueprints are arriving from Heaven. God is assigning spiritual cartographers who will bring new clarity, understanding, and simplicity to our mission. Like the disciples in Jerusalem, God is asking us to look to beyond natural borders to see all of Earth as His Kingdom.

Creating Apostolic Communities

Creating an apostolic community will challenge our existing thinking and our current structures of ministry. The mission of the Church is big and requires big thinkers. Apostolic leaders will disrupt comfort levels. They gather around mission instead of preferences. They help differentiate between the essentials and non-essentials.

Historically, movements have gathered and formed around a common theology or a shared experience. But over time, these movements encounter pitfalls. Unless they are challenged and corrected, people will keep living and working in the same rut, producing the same results. Here are a few of those pitfalls:

- We protect the past at the expense of the future.
- We take ownership instead of stewardship.
- We only gather around people who think the same way we think.
- We build defensive systems to protect our group against any challenge.
- We shut out new ways of thinking, new personnel, and new vision.
- We fail to institute systems that honestly evaluate our effectiveness.
- We ignore the real issues and carry on with business as usual.

What makes this organizational shift toward an apostolic environment so difficult? Difficulty arises when we define how we do church as fixed and rigid. We start to see any challenge to our self-defined sacredness as a threat or a compromise, and we dismiss the potential of something new. Challenges get marginalized or eliminated from the discussion, and we stop moving forward. Sometimes, the very message God wants to deliver is carried by a person or an idea we consider threatening.

We are deceived if we think we don't need to continually change and reform. A shift requires adjustments in our beliefs and our thinking. These changes never toss out our core beliefs, but they do simplify our thinking and keep us mobile and not entrenched in a partial understanding of a much larger truth. Healthy corrections and adjustments will change the way see our friendship with God. With a more mature love, we will be able to live a simple faith that has the ability to transform culture because it first transformed us.

Cutting Away the Fat

One night almost thirty years ago, I was flying in a small plane with my pastor, Roy Hicks, Jr. It was about 2:00 a.m., and Roy and I were flying all night to get back to Los Angeles after a weeklong conference in North Carolina.

As we droned deeper into the ink-black night sky, I asked Roy a question somewhere over Mississippi: "Roy, if tomorrow you found yourself leading our denomination, what would you do?" Roy paused and then answered: "I would do away with a lot of our structure, take our available funds and resources and give them to fifty lighthouse churches in fifty states, and let them do what God had called them to do."

The phrase, "lighthouse church," was Roy-speak for a church led by an apostolic leader. Apostles cut away the unnecessary bulk and blockages that people, local churches, or denominations tend to accumulate over the years. That cutting away is like a skilled butcher removing unnecessary fat from a fine cut of meat.

This cutting away makes those in control of existing systems nervous because they themselves may be some of the fat destined for cuts made by the spiritual butcher's knife. If you are faced with the task of making these cuts, do it with honor and sensitivity. Just because someone is part of the current problem does not mean they do not have a place in a future reformation if they are willing to allow God to intervene. Each person has value in God's Kingdom.

Planned Communities

When I was a kid growing up in California, the phrase, "Planned Community" was coined. A planned community is created on a plot of undeveloped land. It is designed and built from scratch.

Some of these communities were built out in the desert where there were only jackrabbits and sagebrush. Planners laid out each city street and assigned house plots and addresses. Everything was developed with the plan in mind.

As we revisit the concept of a community led by apostolic vision and its vital role in reformation, we need to go back to the original training and equipping Paul addressed in Ephesians 4. In that original plan, each of the five equipping gifts function like drafting tools God will use to create the blueprint for a planned community of faith.

Living in community is healthiest when we know our own street address and how to find our way home again. The job of apostolic leadership is to make sure each generation understands God's original blueprint and where each of us fits.

Paving a New Roadway

Jan and I were driving north on Interstate 5 in Oregon when we entered a construction zone. We slowed and formed a single lane of traffic as directed by an electronic road sign. On the other side of the freeway, a large paving machine was inching its way forward, laying down a new roadway. At the time, I felt the Lord ask me to make a note about the paving machine. He would tell me later what it meant.

That evening, I revisited the note I had recorded earlier. Immediately, the Lord revealed an image. I saw the paving machine jump its track and leave the surveyed roadbed. It started to pave in a new and unanticipated direction.

Most of us have planned and surveyed how we thought our lives would work out. That plan was our roadway. But the road we've traveled has become old and worn, no longer able to bear the weight of future transport. It carried us to this point, but it's beyond the point of repair. It needs to be replaced. We relied more on tradition and assumption than following the innovative track of the Holy Spirit. We operated too much out of our own strength and reasoning. Something is changing. New roads of faith are being cut because new instruction is being heard.

Some of you have heard the sound of a prophet's voice announcing that a new way is being paved. The sound of that voice has caught your ear. You are being invited to come and examine a new blueprint for your personal life and for your assignment in your profession or job skill.

The Lord has plans for us that will require building a new roadway rather than just filling in the potholes and smoothing over the ruts of our current path. We will become like the paving machine I saw on the freeway. In a time of reformation, God will have us leave the known route and go in an unexpected direction. This is a courageous assignment. Those who move in these new directions are the people we read about in the annals of Church history.

The Spark of Reformation

Researchers at Northwestern University have discovered that when a sperm and egg unite, a zinc-colored spark of light ignites at the moment of conception. This was a stunning and unexpected discovery.

You were physically born with a spark of light. When you received the life of Christ, you were spiritually born again with that same creative light. You have been called to an ever-increasing manifestation of that light until the day your physical body dies. The One who is the light of all life will someday welcome you into the greater light of eternity illuminated by the very presence of Jesus.

Whenever any form of God's creativity takes place, there is light. The process of creation recorded in Genesis included the words of the Creator: "Let there be light." Creativity and spiritual freedom come when the light of God's truth illuminates a target for a creative act. The Word of God is described as a lamp to our feet and a light to our path.

Your whole life is a record of the effects of God's light. Allow the reality of His spark of light to create confidence when you face a dark moment. His illumination will guide you through every dark alley of life. The darkness before you will have to yield to the light inside you. The light you carry is the evidence that death no longer has a place of victory in you.

Your understanding of who you are will need to be challenged by light. You were designed to function as a burning one: consumed by love and pouring out love around you. You are an illuminating presence. If you have allowed yourself to burn down and become just a dim ember, God has a word for you. It is similar to the word Paul gave Timothy when he admonished him to stir up the gifts already imparted to him. May the breath of God blow on you and ignite your passion once again.

The wisdom of Proverbs will become more evident the deeper you experience a reformation and return to God's original intentions for you. Your life will become "like the first gleam of dawn, which shines ever brighter until the full light of day" (Proverbs 4:18). Things are getting brighter!

Recovering Lost Treasure

I remember the first time I heard the phrase, "glacial moraine." A friend of mine who was a PhD candidate in the field of geology came to visit Jan and me. We were struggling young pastors trying to plant our first church in Kalispell, Montana. He was an experienced pastor and brought us the encouragement and wisdom we needed to go on.

While on a drive through Glacier Park, my friend pointed out a large field of gravel-like rubble called a glacial moraine. The moraine spread from the base of a large ice field. A moraine is the crushed rock and debris left behind in the migration path of a moving slab of glacial ice. Some of these fields of glacial moraine were a mile long. It looked like a commercial rock-crushing machine had worked its way down the mountain, uncovering what had been hidden out of sight.

I enjoy a Facebook page called "Secrets of the Ice." Due to the recession of glaciers around the world, teams of archaeologists are being sent to these glaciers to recover what is being unearthed before the artifacts are taken by relic-hunters. The teams are discovering previously unknown archaeological treasures that would have remained a secret unless revealed by the receding ice field.

In one article, a photo showed an archaeologist holding a very well-preserved arrow. It was at least a thousand years old and yet fully intact. The point, shaft, and feathers were all present. It had somehow survived under the weight of the ice after all these years. The arrow was alone and not in a quiver. It was most likely shot and lost in the snow during a hunt.

In the rubble of our history, we will discover treasures that have been long forgotten and considered lost. For the Church, the unearthing of our history will confirm a treasure: the previous existence of a simpler faith that has been lost under the slow-moving glacier of religion.

After reading the article, I was drawn to read Elisha's account in II Kings 13. Elisha was getting ready to die, and the king of Israel had come to visit the old prophet. Elisha told the king to shoot an arrow through an open window toward the east as a prophetic act, signifying victory in upcoming battles with the Syrians who had been oppressing Israel.

Then Elisha told the king to strike the ground with his remaining handful of arrows. The king only hit the ground three times. Elisha became upset, telling the king he should have continued hitting the ground. Only three strikes indicated a limited faith and a lack of enthusiasm for what might have seemed like a foolish act to the king.

The king had faith to shoot the first arrow through the window. He did not have much faith for striking the ground with the arrows from his quiver. This was the more imaginative prophetic act that didn't make as much sense. The King's limited imagination also limited the scope of his future victories. Just as Elisha prophesied, the king won only three battles against his enemies.

Some of us are like the king. We received a word from Scripture or a prophetic word. We shot our arrow through a window of faith, not yet seeing the full significance of our act of obedience. In doing so, we affirmed what God wanted to do for us. But we did not match that prophetic act with a corresponding measure of faith.

The history of the Church is littered with these shortsighted responses. Like the king, we limit God's ability to assist us in a battle by stopping short in the continued exercise of our faith. God has a plan for a much larger victory and we need corresponding acts of faith to signify our agreement with His plan.

God is asking us to shoot His arrows of redemption into all the nations of the world. He has a large and expansive plan to bring freedom to all who have been oppressed. His redemptive plan can include the return of a wayward child, the restoration of a broken relationship, the creation of a thriving business, the placement of a just government, safe neighborhoods, honorable educational systems, and nations offering their citizens the love of God. God intends His redemptive acts to be experienced by everyone in every setting, without limit or qualification.

God is also asking us to stay steady and keep contending. Our willingness to obey His voice will determine the degree of our victories. Like the archaeologist who discovered the treasure of an ancient arrow lost long ago, you too will discover deeply buried treasures that are part of your future assignment. These forgotten treasures will be unearthed by the Spirit in this generation. This is how reformation begins.

The treasure of God's plan has been buried and preserved. It was never lost—just hidden for revelation in this time of reformation. Pick up the arrow and shoot it once again. Take all the arrows from your quiver of promise and, in faith, begin to strike the ground of your inheritance. Prophesy hope over your family, your church, your workplace, your city, your region, your nation, and do not stop until God says to stop. If you choose to live at this level of faith, you will see God win battles you never thought possible. The generations after you will benefit from these victories because of your acts of faith.

Making the Exchange

Jan and I were part of a conference in Bend, Oregon—a beautiful part of the country. The host church provided a warm and hospitable place for all of us to gather.

In the pre-service meet-and-greet time, hundreds of us mingled for casual conversation in the atrium of the church. I was able to connect with people I had not seen in years. During some of the conversations that took place, I saw in the Spirit the word "Exchange" hanging over several of the pastors and their spouses.

Later that night, I lay in bed in the darkness praying for the coming day. As I reviewed the images of exchange I had seen earlier that day, I immediately knew what the Lord was saying. For the last thirty-six years of ministry, Jan and I entered each new season having made an exchange. In one season, we exchanged betrayal for a deeper trust in God and an appropriate trust in others. At another time, we exchanged a reliance on well-meaning church programs for a display of the raw and unpredictable power of God. Every new season began with an exchange. In every season of life, we are given the opportunity to exchange our weakness for God's strength.

After the death, resurrection, and enthronement of Jesus, He gave us everything upfront pertaining to our salvation as a gift of grace. We now have the opportunity to live in the fullness of that deposit. To experience those things, we have to come into agreement with Him. He doesn't force His agenda on us. For each exchange, we have to be willing to let go of something old in order to take hold of something new.

God asks us to give Him the things that fill our hands with false promise and the illusion of control. It is too easy to think we can make life work without a full dependence on Him. With empty hands we become candidates for something new and wonderful—something beyond our ability to fully comprehend. With empty hands we can take hold of His love, joy, peace, hope, and everything that pertains to living in the fullness of Christ.

At each crossroads of life, you will be asked to make an exchange. The exchange might be the way you think, the way you do church, or how you see your place in culture. Reformation belongs to those who are willing to make these exchanges.

FIVE

Looking for Gold

Your chosen profession or job skill will give you a place to stand on the Seven Mountains of culture. You don't need the Spirit to do these jobs, but you do need the Spirit to help you demonstrate and speak God's truth in love while you fulfill the tasks associated with your work.

Your voice has been created to speak to the institutions, groups, and individuals who currently control the sound emanating from each mountain. The voice of a CEO can be used to alter the atmosphere in a Fortune 500 boardroom moments before an important business decision is made. The truth spoken in love can change the relationship between a parent and child in a tense family crisis. The sound of Heaven released by a country singer can change the mood in a lounge during a weekend gig.

It is not enough to just perform a job. When the Holy Spirit releases the sound of Heaven, your voice tunes to the unique frequency used by God to declare His truth and express His limitless love.

Some of the challenges we are currently facing as a culture were birthed in a time of silence when the voice of the Church was not heard on the mountains of culture. As I mentioned before, we have often limited our voice of influence to religion and family. That limitation effectively removed the voice of the Church from a place of significance in culture. In many cases, the only sound we have made has been a corrective sound spoken in defensive tones. Those sounds do not produce life—they only create distance and separation.

We've been assigned by God to call out the gold embedded in people. We have a mission to speak the truth in love; to tell the people that God created them in love, for love; to tell them the beautiful details about their true identity.

A declaration of God's heart is waiting to be heard on assembly lines, in gift shops, and within the halls of Congress. No place is off limits to our voice of redemption. Words of truth spoken in love become a spiritual prospecting tool that can dig out the hidden gold in people.

Have you been looking for a model for reformation? There really isn't a single model. In fact, I do not believe any absolute model or magic formula exists. In our search for these models, we have only created well-worn paths around the mountain of religion. God is releasing a fresh blueprint for the Church. It is fresh to us because we have lived so long with a broken adaptation of the original blueprint that anything new is like a fresh breath of spiritual wind.

If you are afraid of change, take heart. It will all work out if you are willing to let go of your idea of what the Church is supposed to look like and allow God to build it. A spiritual structure will not work well when it is rigidly fused. It needs to be built with flexibility and examined often for authenticity and relevance.

God's Word is a two-edged sword cutting deep into the marrow of our presumptions. This is where the most profound works of reformation take place.

Some of us are so far away from what the Lord intended, that if the original model suddenly appeared, we would label it "Off Limits!" Be careful with labels. Once we label a person or group or a move of God, all effective conversation will cease. Instead, our calling is to be a voice of invitation to something beautiful.

Binocular Vision

When I was a young pastor living in Montana, a mountain man befriended me. He taught me how to work an open canoe through Fool Hen Rapids on the North Fork of the Flathead River and how to hunt in the mountains and valleys of Northwest Montana.

One day this friend asked, "Do you have a good set of binoculars?" I said, "Yes, my dad gave me his." My friend walked with me deep into the forest and said, "See that stand of dense timber? Use your binoculars to find the deer." I thought he was nuts. Binoculars work great on the open plains where you need to see for miles, but not here in heavy brush and timber.

My friend took a few moments to explain how binoculars work. He showed me how I could focus my binoculars on the first line of trees. Then using the focus knob on the top of the binoculars, he moved the area of focus back into the stand of trees. One after another, I moved each narrow slice of focus deeper into the forest until I was about fifty feet inside the tree line. It was then that I saw the eye of a deer. Not the whole body. Not the complete head, just a single eye looking back at me.

I was amazed. I dropped the binoculars to my chest and said, "I would never have imagined this was possible." We let the little doe trot off into the depths of the forest unharmed. The focus function of the binoculars taught me a valuable lesson.

When Jesus birthed the Church, He founded us on a really simple model. That model is His redemptive love. Love is our narrow field of focus, like moving the focus of my binoculars deeper into the forest to gain new perspective and clarity. The branches and twigs no longer blurred my vision because they were out of my narrow area of focus.

Focus is only possible with simplicity. Simplicity can help us see the way forward through all the obstacles set before us. In the process of finding our point of focus, we will discover what is hidden deep within the complexity of our diverse culture.

If speaking the truth in love is the simple product of our equipping and maturing, any follower of Christ can use that focus of love to train their eyes on what truly matters. When any of this gets overly complicated, our faith becomes blurred, blinding us to what lies hidden. Reformation helps us find our focus and, in some cases, to discover focus for the first time.

Jesus: The New Wineskin

As I prepared the manuscript for this book, I saw the image of a knothole in a pine board. I saw two seasons in the life of the Church. Two very different realities existed on either side of the board. The knothole was our place of passage into reformation. It would lead us from something old into something new. I saw people trying to pull old and brittle wineskins through the knothole. The old wineskins were not able pass through. They began to break and shatter in the effort. Then I saw a supple and pliable wineskin being easily pulled through the knothole of reformation.

For many years, I have read about wineskins described as new and creative models of ministry. There is nothing wrong with that metaphor as long as we understand the original intent of what Jesus was saying. In Luke 5, Jesus was telling His listeners that He is the new wineskin. He came to fulfill and replace the wineskin of an old and expired covenant. He is the container for the new wine of a new covenant.

> *And no one puts new wine into old wineskins. For the new wine would burst the wineskins, spilling the wine and ruining the skins. New wine must be stored in new wineskins. But no one who drinks the old wine seems to want the new wine. "The old is just fine," they say* (Luke 5:37-39).

The teachers of Jesus' day were demanding that He and His disciples fit into an old wineskin of a Law-based covenant that was passing away. They were saying by their life and theology, "The old is good enough." Jesus was illustrating that the structure of the

98

old covenant would not be able to contain the freshness of the new and expanding Kingdom represented by His life. It would not pass through the knothole. A new spiritual container was required to hold a new covenant—not an old and brittle wineskin of the past.

Jesus is our wineskin. At the moment of our salvation, we became a new creation—a completely new wineskin capable of containing the expanding effects of the new wine of a new Kingdom. We are living wineskins of God's increasing grace, not some tired and expired wineskin of the Law, no longer able to contain the capacity of new life.

Regarding leaving behind the old wineskin of the Law, Apostle Paul said in his letter to the Philippians: "For His sake I have discarded everything else, counting it all as garbage, so that I could gain Christ and become one with Him" (3:8b-9).

In the context of that chapter, Paul first listed his significant Jewish pedigree in the Law. Then he says he threw it all away for Christ. He was discarding the former wineskin to become one with the new wineskin—Jesus.

If we describe our life as something new and culturally relevant, and then call it "a new wineskin," that is fine as long as our model was first formed by the life of Christ. Jesus didn't come to create models of ministry. Those will adjust and morph over time. He came to hand out new wineskins filled with His presence, and those new wineskins will represent what reformation looks like in each generation of the Church.

When Jesus rose from the dead and sat down on His throne at the right hand of the Father, He sent His Spirit to put the sound of Heaven into our mouths. *That* is our model for ministry. Every time we open our mouths and speak the truth in love, the wine of Heaven is poured out.

Once we have a healthy understanding of new wineskins, our experience will look like the birthday party in John 2 when the host ran out wine, and Jesus turned water into wine. Our celebration and creativity will be an invitation that will attract the world to the goodness of God's free-flowing supply of new wine.

Watching the Hand of God

About four years after planting our first church, I had become tired and disillusioned. It got so bad I was ready to call it quits. Along with pastoring our young church, I worked as a flight instructor. I told Jan I felt it was time to quit pastoring and relocate with my transferrable trade as a pilot. Jan asked me a few questions for which I had no real answers. In silent wisdom, she allowed me to play out what was taking place in my heart.

We drove from Kalispell, Montana to Portland, Oregon to check on flying jobs. I was offered a job as a pilot and made plans to return in a month. Flying for a living sounded so much better than the stress I was experiencing as a pastor. The church was actually doing well. We were growing and had a wonderful sense of community, but I was worn out. Tired pastors don't make healthy decisions, and I had just made one of those decisions.

I returned to Kalispell and planned to meet with our leadership team to let them know what I had decided to do. Before the meeting, I shared my decision with my brother, Dwain. He said, "That doesn't sound like God." In my mind, I thought, "Wait a minute, little brother. You are a contractor, and I am the pastor. This is my area of expertise, not yours." My brother was right, and I was dead wrong.

I then called a close friend of mine, Stan Simmons, who pastored a wonderful church in Billings, Montana. I shared my story with Stan. His reply came from Psalm 123:2 (NASB):

Behold, as the eyes of servants look to the hand of

their master,
As the eyes of a maid to the hand of her mistress,
So our eyes look to the Lord our God....

Stan's wisdom and my brother's word of caution made me realize I was running away from my problem, not engaging it. I called the owner of the flight company who had graciously offered me a job and declined the offer. I canceled the meeting with my leaders and decided to let God—not my emotions—direct my next steps.

In that time, I learned another valuable lesson. Healthy decisions are never made in isolation. I had isolated myself from the input of others and set in motion a sad series of decisions that could have delayed or even derailed the wonderful life Jan and I now enjoy.

As you experience your own personal reformation, add to your process conversations with trusted friends. In those shared conversations, you may find they have gone through similar journeys. Their wisdom may save you from making a sad mistake. A prophetic word of encouragement spoken in truth and love will help introduce maturity to any decision-making process.

A sense of shared community is one of the hallmarks of maturity. The lone ranger mentality has been exposed for the lie it is. As a young and insecure leader, I was afraid that the exposure of my fatigue and disillusionment would display an image of weak leadership. Just the opposite is true. People want to share in our struggles. A community called to speak the truth in love will provide a place where we can demonstrate to each other the love of God in tender and practical ways. We prepare ourselves for reformation by living a known life, not a hidden one.

Go Back and Do What's in the Book

After my failed attempt at running away, I went back to pastoring and settled in with the hope that God would reveal our next step. That next step took place a few months later when Jan and I traveled to Los Angeles to hear John Wimber, the leader of the Vineyard movement, speak at the historic Angelus Temple.

I remember watching Wimber walk out onto the platform. He was wearing a bright Hawaiian shirt and white pants. He had a gray beard, and he looked like an island version of Santa Claus. Early in his sermon he said, "I am just a little fat guy trying to get to Heaven." His image and humor disarmed me and set me up to hear a bit of life-transforming advice. At one point in his sermon, Wimber said, "Go back to your church and just do what's in the Book." I didn't hear anything else. Those twelve words were why God had sent us to the conference. I had my God-deposit. We flew back home in time for our Sunday service.

We changed nothing that first Sunday back in Kalispell. The same worship team played the same worship songs. I had a sermon already prepared to preach. It was all the same except for one huge change; hope and expectation had filled my heart.

When worship began, so did the miracles. No one called for a prayer line. The Spirit simply began to breathe on us as we worshipped the Lord. After the service, one of our leaders came up to me and said, "What happened to you? You came back changed. I can hear it in your voice." I *had* changed. I came back with a simplicity of mission that only hope and expectation can provide.

Over the next few months, we continued to see significant diseases and physical deformities healed. Forgiveness was granted. Relationships were restored. God's love was tangible. We were making a place for what was in the Book. By the timing of the Holy Spirit, revival had come to our little town. With it came a refreshing sense of purpose.

God sent us to Los Angeles to hear a man who would challenge us. An impartation of faith took place from a man whose obedience rekindled our spirits. We carried that fire back home. Our reception to the Word put us in position to receive far beyond anything we expected. Our mustard seed of faith opened a miraculous window to the people we were called to shepherd, and God began to release Heaven's blessing upon us.

I learned that a personal reformation always precedes a larger corporate reformation in churches, nations, and culture. If you want to see God move on a larger scale, make sure you are asking Him to do that same work in you. Once you are reformed and revitalized, you will walk back into your familiar surroundings as a change agent for His glory.

Pliable Thinking

We have to become pliable if we are going to participate with God to usher in reformation. This is a pliability of our heart that will eventually affect the way we think.

Psalms 37:4 says, "Delight yourself in the Lord; and He will give you the desires of your heart" (NASB). When I researched the words *delight* and *desires*, I discovered something interesting. Delight can be translated "to be pliable" and desires can be translated as "a request."

We can start out thinking we know what we want, like I did as a young pastor. (That didn't work for me.) We have another option. We can put our life in God's hands and let Him make us pliable. God will begin to rework our broken thinking to come into line with His heart and mind.

Once we become pliable, our thinking will be transformed to such a degree that our desires will actually change in the process. These new desires will create entirely new requests of God.

Until we become pliable, our desires will only reflect an old mindset of brittle wineskins, which cannot pass through knotholes of transition and will continue to break apart. The sad result will be that culture will look at us and ask, "Why would I want that?"

Instead, we will have the opportunity to model new wineskins that will reflect the beauty of Heaven on Earth.

SIX

Apostolic Motherhood

Family is one of the Seven Mountains of cultural influence. It is important, and yet aspects of it have not been treated as important. It's time to rethink many of the traditional roles we love and honor, including the role of motherhood. The mountains of government, religion, business, education, media, and arts & entertainment seem more powerful and culture-altering than family. It is a mistake to think that way. A powerful woman lives on the mountain of family: her name is mom.

I was recently teaching on the Seven Mountains when the Lord dropped an unscripted thought into my heart about the role of mothers on the mountain of family. What I am writing will also apply to fathers, but the Lord wanted me to specifically highlight mothers.

Motherhood has been relegated to what some see as a, "tuck the kids into bed, bake the cake, and clean a kid's snotty nose" kind of job. For sure, a loving mother will do many of those kinds of things, but she does significantly more.

If you are a mom, I want to challenge you to see yourself in a different context. You have the potential to become a one-woman apostolic sending agency. Every child you raise has a Kingdom assignment on one of the Seven Mountains of culture. You are significant and so is your calling.

For those of you who will become mothers, from the moment you discover that you are carrying a child within you, begin to build up their spirit. Welcome them to life. Speak prophetically over their future. Bless them and declare their heritage to displace the lies they will hear so often. Cultivate their identity with your words. As they grow, support their education and training to prepare them to release the passion God births in their heart. You have been called to raise children with a Kingdom mindset and send them out to influence society.

Moms who are able to understand this unique assignment are dangerous to darkness, and hell knows it. You will take hits from people who see you only as the soccer-team chauffeur, your family's domestic arm, or the woman who left her dreams at the wedding altar. You are more! We honor your vital role in developing a generation who will transform the Seven Mountains of culture.

Prophetic Artists

My daughter, Anna, is a writer and artist. She was trained and educated in both disciplines. Anna was awarded a Fulbright Scholarship and lived in Europe as a poet. God has blessed the work of her hands.

I remember the day in our apartment in Berlin, Germany when Anna sat down with me to develop a long-range vision for her life. We discussed a plan to merge her passions of writing and art into a single discipline. From that place she could train, raise, and release writers and artists from a shared passion. She even saw herself owning a residential training center where she could invite artists and writers from all over the world to explore creative dimensions of word and art.

Today, twenty years after that time in Berlin, Anna is fulfilling her dream. She works with very creative and wonderful people. She navigates with grace and dignity into varied environments and cultures with people from all walks of life. We see God's favor upon her.

Each year Anna leads prophetic art workshops in the US and overseas. She also helps lead workshops to nations like Nepal, Spain, Morocco, and Mexico that train people to expand their writing and storytelling ability. Her art hangs in galleries all over the world. It has been a joy to watch Anna make the creative sounds of God's love in her sphere of influence.

Evangelic Dentistry

At a conference in Albany, Oregon, I met a husband and wife team who led us in worship. This couple ministers in a variety of settings. Worshipping with them makes you feel as if you are sitting near the throne of God listening to angels sing.

Jan and I had lunch with them and others who were ministering at the conference. The wife told us how her father, a dentist, would use his office as a place to share the love of God with his clients. His appointments would often run over time because a patient was meeting Jesus.

This man's love and compassion were so influential that at his death, his memorial service drew a huge crowd from around the region to honor his life. Many people told stories of the impact he made in his community. He took the sound of God's love outside the walls of the Church into the place of his profession, and he changed a community.

God is releasing many of us to see a much larger picture of God's Kingdom that exists outside the walls of tradition and our narrow understanding of ministry. The truth spoken in love can no longer be isolated to the mountain of religion. Its fullest expression is destined to be heard in all spheres of culture.

Pastoring Corporations

At the same conference, I met another husband and wife. The husband is a physician who is part of a team of 1,500 professionals. They make up the physician pool in a large medical corporation. The wife is the pastor of a new church plant. Both are comfortable in their different roles.

During a conversation with this couple, I discovered something very powerful taking place in the medical corporation where the husband works. He wanted to introduce the concept made notable in Danny Silk's book, *Culture of Honor*. This physician wanted to find ways for the corporation to walk in honor with its employees and clients. He was inspired to use his voice to make a difference in his place of business.

The doctor told me he was not able to use the name of Jesus in his endeavor, but that did not stop him. He approached the board of the corporation and shared with them the importance and value of honor in the organization. After hearing his well-crafted presentation, the board gave him permission to implement training to create a culture of honor. He is essentially pastoring a corporate community.

Marketplace Teachers

When we think of a teacher, we normally think of someone in a classroom or behind a pulpit. But there are other kinds of teachers who educate in unconventional settings.

Shortly after writing one of my books, *God-Whispers*, I was approached by a man I had known in years past. John and I reconnected when he contacted me and asked how he could purchase a large order of my books to give away.

John had been very successful in the medical field and had retired early. He was not one to sit around. John had a gift to teach others about God, and he found unique places to share his gift of teaching. The Lord had John teach in a prison, as a chaplain for a minor league professional baseball team, and with corporate executives in boardroom settings.

God-Whispers is a collection of several hundred proverbial statements about life and our relationship with God. John commented to me when he was ordering the books, "I like the simple one-liners in the book. Men can quickly capture these statements and easily process a concept of God." John would take a proverb from the book and ask the men he was teaching what it meant to them. He would then use the men's insights as a starting point to teach them about a loving, heavenly Father and how to live an honorable life.

The deepest needs of the men in prisons, on baseball teams, or in corporate boardrooms are the same. They all need someone to teach them about the love of God and how to translate that love into their everyday lives and relationships.

The coming reformation will tap a diverse pool of non-traditional teachers who will venture into new and unexplored places of ministry. Some of the most impactful teachers in this reformation will not be formally trained. They will be people who began to walk in obedience to the nudge of the Spirit. As a result of their obedience, God will open unusual doors for the release of their gift.

SEVEN

Keep Flying in Faith

In my years as a pilot, I also flew charter flights. On one of those charters, I was flying back to our home base in Kalispell, Montana after dropping off a client in Great Falls.

I was flying a Piper Arrow, a high-performance, single-engine aircraft. Piloting in Montana through the Rocky Mountains requires that you pay special attention to the weather; it can change in an instant. If you don't treat weather with respect, you could become a statistic in a National Transportation Safely Board incident report.

Prior to departure, I paid a visit to the Flight Service Station (FSS) at the Great Falls Airport. I discussed the current weather with a staff member. The large windows of the FSS offered a clear view toward Rogers Pass, through which I would need to fly. This route would take me over Lincoln, Montana up the Swan Valley, and into Kalispell. As the FSS person and I talked, we looked out at the distant mountain pass. I asked about the current cloud ceiling. He said, "It looks like it will hold." With that, I left the building, conducted my pre-flight check, and took off for home.

The departure was normal. I had enough cloud clearance to safely and legally fly. As I approached Rogers Pass, it was still a go. I slipped through the pass, and then my world changed—dramatically. After entering the Pass, the clouds began to descend, sealing off the Pass and preventing me from turning back. I was committed to a scary reality I had not anticipated. An intense snowstorm started, and heavy snow began to fall. I was pressed lower and lower until I was literally less than 100 feet off the valley floor. I couldn't file an instrument flight plan. I was stuck. The small airports along my route of flight were all buried under several feet of snow.

My only option was to follow the highway that traced the turning, twisting, narrow, valley floor along my route. On a clear day and as the crow flies, it was about 150 miles home. On this road-bound snowy flight I would travel over 230 miles and fly at almost half the speed of my normal flight plan.

When the snow first hit, I dropped my landing gear and flaps to slow the aircraft down so that I could pick my way through the storm. During one stretch of the flight, I was down to just 50 feet above ground level. What helped me stay on course and keep flying was the fact that I had driven this route in a car many times before and knew how and where the road twisted and turned.

That morning, the local sheriff's department received a call from a concerned woman whose house was buzzed by a low flying aircraft. The dear woman heard me fly so low over her house in such an intense snowstorm that she was sure a crash had taken place.

I continued flying for over two hours, ranging in altitude from 50 to 100 feet above the snowy terrain. My forward visibility was little more than what I could see immediately below and just in front of me.

The most dangerous part of the flight was a large radio tower a few miles from home. It was twice as tall as the altitude I was currently flying and hidden in the snow and clouds just ahead of me. I could easily hit the tower unless I changed my position at the right time. As I approached the location where I knew the tower was located, I moved to the other side of the roadway opposite the tower. In the next moment, the tower passed by as a blur in the falling snow.

I landed safely and went home to my family. Had I not known the roadway in such great detail, that storm would likely have ended my life.

I had started that journey with experience and wisdom—my own and that of the FSS person, but I ended up trapped in a life-and-death struggle. I was reduced to a single course of action: keep flying the airplane. Flight instructors repeat those words, "keep flying the airplane," to each new pilot they train. Pilots have died in storms because they gave up even when the aircraft was still faithfully flying.

You may have started out on the current leg of your journey into reformation by taking all the possible pre-flight precautions. But something happened that trapped you in a single course of action, and you may have crossed a point of no return. You are in the middle of a storm, and your only option is to keep flying.

Your journey may get really dangerous, but you have the ability to navigate the emotional and spiritual terrain hidden in the clouds along your route. You have been this way before in good weather. You know the road. Keep flying even though what was familiar is now hidden from your sight. Entrusting yourself to God is your only way to be delivered safely to your destination.

Finding Safe Passage

Most of the time, we move forward in faith, but sometimes faith can ask us to wait on the timing of God. I live in the coastal mountain range of Southern Oregon. Parts of this region have become a death trap in the winter to unsuspecting travelers.

With the advent of map apps on smart phones and in-car navigational systems, people are relying more and more on technology to find their way around road closures during winter storms. These map apps can find secondary roads through the mountains that are great to travel during the summer. But in winter, these roads are often covered in deep snow that can trap motorists in remote areas, miles from rescue. Some travelers have not returned from these fatal detours.

This happened again last winter when a monster storm dropped record snowfall in our area. Several cars became stranded near the summit when they attempted to take a detour on a secondary road after the freeway was closed. Thankfully, they were all rescued.

There is a spiritual application to this map-app issue. Reformation is taking place. Be sure to investigate and test what is offered to you with the wisdom of the Word, the leading of the Spirit, and wise counsel. Do not necessarily trust routes that worked in a past season. Reformation requires a new level of faith.

God will become your most trusted traveling companion in the storms of change that have been moving across the spiritual landscape. When you see others taking routes meant for other seasons, you might be tempted to join them. There are times when waiting and trusting will be your safest course of action until you hear a clear word from the Lord. In some cases, waiting will save you from heartache and disappointment. Everything God has promised for you in this time of reformation has been made secure. Let that knowledge give you peace in the passage.

Spiritual Transformers

Understanding what it means to belong to God—to really know Him—is the starting point for discovering our true identity. With that discovery, we can understand our purpose in life.

Finding the perfect spouse will not bring you peace or happiness. Having children will not heal a broken marriage. Electing your favorite politician will not change a nation. Getting the perfect job will not provide security. Even a perfectly bundled theology cannot give you what you really need out of life. Only God can provide what you really need.

A real challenge for a new creation is to begin *thinking* like a new creation. Changing the way we think is one of the greatest miracles we can experience. Once we make that change, all the rest—the search for a perfect spouse, having kids, the false hope of politics, the illusion of a perfect job, and all the rest of life's pursuits—will finally find a healthy place on the list of priorities.

Once you have repositioned these things beneath the transforming work of God, they can be enjoyed for their intended purpose without misdirecting *your* purpose.

Those who are walking in intimacy with God will have been conditioned to hear the subtle inflections of the voice of the Spirit. They will be able to move forward unhindered when rapid change is taking place because they are in tune with the One who knows the way forward.

The Two Doorways

In each reformation of the Church, two doorways will appear: one door is labeled fear and the other door is faith. The door of fear is framed with the rigid familiarity of a religious spirit and the fear of judgment. Anyone who challenges the status quo in this doorway is suspect, and many so-called heretics have been burned at the stake in this doorway. This doorway can sound very spiritual, but when you enter it, it can kill you.

The door of faith is framed with the hope that something good exists beyond our current reality. Passage through this door brings resurrection and new life. The door of faith will invite us to take hold of something new and better and to risk the resulting change. To cross its threshold, we have to open our hands and let go of our unchallenged assumptions.

Fear holds on—even to what is false. Fear produces a death-grip. Faith invites us to let go of the assumptions we have that can hinder a greater revelation of God's heart. We need the revelations of a life of faith to enter into the new future promised in a process of reformation. Letting go is never a threat to the secure foundations of our faith. It is only a threat to the presence of fear.

When Jan and I transitioned out of pastoring a local church into our current assignment, we were expectant. We had been through many transitions before, both large and small. As it was in each transition, the doorways of fear and faith appeared. Having been this way before, we did not hesitate to step through the door of faith knowing the fear of loss was simply a well-crafted lie.

We have never looked back in regret, even though we each experienced unexpected physical challenges while the change was taking place. We were shaken— but not from our forward motion in faith. Our emotional and spiritual shaking exposed our never-ending battle with fear. Fear was not able to stand in the presence of faith. Fear is the opposite of love, and we were being trained once again to go deeper into new dimensions of God's love. In that depth, we discovered the goodness of God as an affirmation that the doorway of faith was the right choice.

You will always face two doorways. No matter what the cost, face your fear but step into the doorway of faith. Entrust yourself to the One who is the author of your faith. He will never leave you or forsake you in your moment of decision. Ask Him to help you turn the knob on the door of faith. When you step across the threshold, you will carry the elements of reformation in your heart. Once you make this passage, nothing will ever be the same again.

Getting Reinvented

Jan and I handed the church we were pastoring over to a great team of young leaders, some of whom had been with us for fifteen years. We commissioned most of them when they were in their early 20's. They had a great deal of maturity even then, and our trust in their integrity has only grown ever since. Watching these men and women grow into their unique styles and callings has been a joy.

During this last transition, Jan and I went through a process of reinvention. God needed to reinvent our thinking. We were taking hold of something new, so we had to also let go of something old. I remember the day when the Lord revealed to me what this would look like. In the Spirit, I saw a large room. In the center of the room was a small, round table. On the table lay three plates, each with a word written on it: writing, teaching, and mentoring. The Lord said, "This is your assignment for the next season of your life."

I was already doing all three of these things while pastoring full-time. After the transition, I no longer had to schedule these assignments around the calendar of a local church or my duties as a pastor. These three assignments would now be what set my calendar and schedule.

Several years have passed since the transition, and the deeper I go into this season's assignment, the more I like the change.

Some people have asked me, "Garris, how do you like retirement?" I wanted to tell them, "I didn't retire. I simply stepped into a new assignment," but I didn't always want to give a corrective reply. Finally, I stopped trying to explain that I had not retired. Now when people ask that question, I simply say, "Life is good!"

My transition has given me large chunks of uninterrupted time to devote to writing. I still teach, but now I teach across a wider variety of faith communities. I spend time with people and churches helping them process transition. I love my life!

All of this change began with an uncomfortable shift in my thinking. I say uncomfortable because it began with a sense of restlessness. This restlessness was actually a Spirit-inspired preparation to help me release one season in order to embrace something new. My transition began with a shift in my thinking. All reformation, whether experienced on a personal level or across the larger global Church, will begin with these shifts.

The Best of Times & the Worst of Times

A revolution of faith is taking place. As this revolution heats up and spills into the streets of religion, it would be wise to confirm that your line of faith is securely set to the anchor of hope. You will need to confirm this connection in order to endure the winds of change that are beginning to blow.

Charles Dickens began his classic book, *A Tale of Two Cities*, with this sentence:

> *It was the best of times, it was the worst of times, it was the age of wisdom, it was the age of foolishness, it was the epoch of belief, it was the epoch of incredulity, it was the season of Light, it was the season of Darkness, it was the spring of hope, it was the winter of despair.*

Dickens was writing of the events that took place in two cities, London and Paris, during the French Revolution. The Church is entering a similar season of revolution. A revolution will precede a reformation.

The Church is currently experiencing a shift that will set the stage for a revolution of faith. Revolutions can be dangerous. Heads roll and entire systems of faith and culture are radically transformed in the process. Don't live in fear at what is taking place. Choose to walk in mature wisdom. Paul said when we walk at this level of maturity, "We will not be influenced when people try to trick us with lies so clever they sound like the truth" (Ephesians 4:14b).

These are the best of times and the worst of times. They are the best of times because God is revealing new aspects of His love and nature to His people. They are the worst of times because some people will choose to believe lies and assume they are truth. As it has been throughout the history of the Church, the lies will deal with the person of Jesus Christ and His plan of redemption for humanity.

Scripture tells us that Jesus Christ is the same yesterday, today, and forever. He never changes. He is your only place of security in a time of revolution when delusions are being offered to you in the name of God.

Prepare yourself for this revolution by pressing deeper into oneness with your God. Intimacy with Him will be your best survival preparation. Soak your heart and mind in the Gospels. Find the scarlet thread of Jesus Christ revealed in the first acts of Creation all the way to the last verse in Revelation.

When Jesus said He was the way, the truth, and the life, "the way" means more than Him being the only way of salvation. He is the only safe way forward through the spiritual bloodshed that a revolution of faith will produce.

Your faith is about to be tested. The test is not a test of disqualification. It will be a test of affirmation, helping you see that the One in whom you have placed your trust will be faithful to bring you through the revolution no matter what takes place. When Jesus is at the center of your being, you are always living in the best of times.

Establishing a Connection

I was teaching a prophetic class in the school of ministry at a wonderful church in Salem, Oregon. When I speak somewhere, my books are usually available for sale. A kind woman from the church offered to manage the book table for me.

After teaching and greeting some of the students, I walked back to the book table. It had been about half an hour since I finished my teaching. The woman working the book table looked troubled. She let me know she had sold a lot of books but was concerned that the credit card sales did not go through. We use a portable credit card reader that simply needs a Wi-Fi signal to operate.

The woman showed me the iPad, and sure enough, it looked like it had not been logged onto the Internet. The woman was afraid that none of the sales had been processed. She began to offer to make it right. I told her that if a mistake had taken place it was just that: a mistake. We would simply assume God was gifting the books to people.

I finally was able to log onto the Internet and checked the status of the sales report. As I checked, one after one, the sales made when the unit was not connected began to appear as completed transactions. The sales were held "somewhere" and finally registered once the connection was made.

Some of you have felt disconnected like my credit card sales system. You have felt disconnected from the results of your labor. Nothing has seemed to register when you prayed. The solutions you hoped for have not materialized. In this time of disconnect, God has not forgotten you. He has kept each prayer and each act of obedience safe and secure in His heart. He has not let them disappear. They have been waiting for release in this time of renewed intimacy with God.

God did not hold these answers back as a form of punishment. When life "happens" and things go sideways—accidently or otherwise—He simply wants you to reconnect with Him at a deeper level of intimacy. When the answers and solutions are finally released, they will begin to flood into your life. Your restored intimacy with God will release the delivery of your acts of faith. Nothing has been lost. Everything will arrive at just the right time.

You may have prayed and believed for years for a reformation to take place in the Church. During that time, it seemed as if nothing was taking place, but God has always been at work. He has been at work aligning people and situations for this moment in history.

Much of this activity has been invisible because it has been taking place in the hearts of people, just like it has been taking place in your heart. When the final connection is made, all the elements will come together, and you will see a great work of God unfold right before you eyes. This is such a good time to be alive!

Your Place of Promise

When I was a kid, my father often took me fishing. One of my favorite ways to fish was with a bobber and worm. A bobber is a small, red-and-white plastic ball fishermen attach to their line a few feet above a dangling worm. The bobber floats on the surface of the water and when the bait is nibbled by a fish, the moving bobber will alert the fisherman that something is taking the bait.

I loved the anticipation the bobber created. On a windy day, when small waves hit the bobber, it would move like a fish was nibbling on the worm. That produced a lot of false alarms and a premature jerking of the pole in an attempt to set the hook on a fish that was not there. On a calm day, the smallest bump of a fish would send out little ripples across the glassy water letting you know a bite was imminent. The ultimate excitement in bobber fishing is when a fish takes a serious bite on the worm and the bobber completely disappears underwater. At that moment, there is no doubt a fish has bitten, and the fight is on.

Some of you have given up on the possibility of a reformation in the Church. You have not seen any activity around your bobber of faith, and you assume that inactivity will continue. You walked away and thought nothing will ever happen. It was like the time I walked away from my bobber after an hour of inactivity. My dad said, "Son, keep your eye on your bobber!" I didn't and went back to the truck. A few minutes later dad yelled, "Garris, you have a fish on!" Down the dirt shore of the lake I ran to find the tip of my pole bouncing up and down and the bobber nowhere in sight. After a few minutes of playing the fighting fish, I landed a nice bass.

Your heavenly Father prefers to have you wait and watch with Him like my father wanted me to do with him. In the waiting, I had the best conversations with my dad. God wants the same kind of time with us.

The promise of a reformation is not the reason He wants us to wait with Him. He wants this time together because He loves being with us.

A fulfilled promise reminds us of His love. The promise will happen. Don't waste that time in worry. Use it to gain a deeper intimacy with the Lord. That intimacy will be the most important guiding presence when you are stepping into the unfamiliar territory that accompanies the moves of God.

His love is so great that even if you have abandoned your place of promise, He will be faithful to call you back when the action starts because He wants to share the excitement of its fulfillment with you. It will be like the day my father let me know a fish was on and my bobber had disappeared. When I finally landed my fish, I looked over at my father. He was smiling and said, "Good job, son!"

This reformation will be something only God can do, but he doesn't want us to miss out. He wants us to share the joy of each other's presence.

A LAST WORD

Throughout this book, I have shared my experience with flying. It has been twenty-five years since I last piloted an airplane. To this day, when a solitary aircraft passes overhead, I look up.

A few years ago, I was out in our backyard with my daughter, Anna. A single-engine airplane droned overhead. I was familiar with that specific sound because I had spent hundreds of hours in an aircraft that sounded that way in flight. I knew it was a Cessna 182. Looking up, I confirmed my guess. I told Anna, "It's a 182."

Some of you are hearing familiar sounds in the Spirit. You know the sound because it has been resonating within you for some time. The sound of this reformation will not pass over you like a distant memory. It wants to pass *through* you to be released as the unique sound of your calling and assignment on the mountains of cultural influence. That sound will be the essence of this reformation.

MINISTRY CONTACT

Garris Elkins
Prophetic Horizons
P.O. Box 509
Jacksonville, Oregon 97530
GarrisElkins.com

Other books by Garris Elkins
available on **amazon.com**:

A Good Place
God-Whispers
The Leadership Rock
Prayers from the Throne of God
The Prophetic Voice
Thoughts to Leave Behind

45495105R00081

Made in the USA
Middletown, DE
05 July 2017